# GODDESSES

# GODDESSES

ANCIENT WISDOM FOR TIMES OF CHANGE FROM OVER 70 GODDESSES

SUE JENNINGS, PH.D.

ILLUSTRATED BY SARAH YOUNG

**HAY HOUSE, INC.**
Carlsbad, California
London • Sydney • Johannesburg
Vancouver • Hong Kong

*To Pauline and Alan, my very special friends, and source of nurture and inspiration.*

**Published and distributed in the United States by:** Hay House, Inc., P.O. Box 5100, Carlsbad, CA 92018-5100 • *Phone:* (760) 431-7695 or (800) 654-5126 • *Fax:* (760) 431-6948 or (800) 650-5115 • www.hayhouse.com • **Published and distributed in Australia by:** Hay House Australia Pty. Ltd., 18/36 Ralph St., Alexandria NSW 2015 • *Phone:* 612-9669-4299 • *Fax:* 612-9669-4144 • www.hayhouse.com.au • **Published and distributed in the United Kingdom by:** Hay House UK, Ltd. • Unit 62, Canalot Studios • 222 Kensal Rd., London W10 5BN • *Phone:* 44-20-8962-1230 • *Fax:* 44-20-8962-1239 • www.hayhouse.co.uk • **Published and distributed in the Republic of South Africa by:** Hay House SA (Pty), Ltd., P.O. Box 990, Witkoppen 2068 • *Phone/Fax:* 2711-7012233 • orders@psdprom.co.za • **Distributed in Canada by:** Raincoast • 9050 Shaughnessy St., Vancouver, B.C. V6P 6E5 • *Phone:* (604) 323-7100 • *Fax:* (604) 323-2600

First published in the UK in 2003 by Vega (ISBN: 1-84333-747-9)

*Design:* Louise Clements
*Illustrations:* Sarah Young

**Library of Congress Control Number:** 2004108771

ISBN 1-4019-0559-5

07 06 05  4 3 2 1
1st U.S. printing, January 2005

Printed in Italy

# Contents

| | A Journey of Wisdom | 6 |
| --- | --- | --- |
| SECTION 1 | An Introduction to the Elements | 8 |
| | Fire | 10 |
| | Water | 24 |
| | Earth | 38 |
| | Air | 52 |
| SECTION 2 | An Introduction to the Heavenly Bodies | 66 |
| | Stars | 68 |
| | Moon | 82 |
| | Sun | 96 |
| SECTION 3 | An Introduction to the Journey of Life | 110 |
| | Triple Goddesses | 112 |
| | Fertility & Childbirth | 126 |
| | Healing | 140 |
| | Creativity & Knowledge | 154 |
| | Journey Through This Book | 168 |
| | Closings and Blessings | 170 |
| | Bibliography | 172 |
| | Index and Acknowledgements | 174 |

**From the Editor:** To our American readers, please note that we have maintained the British spelling, grammar, punctuation, and syntax of the original text in order to preserve the editorial intent of the author (who hails from the United Kingdom).

# A JOURNEY OF *Wisdom*

Before you start reading this book, prepare yourself for a new journey. Be aware that you are thinking about your life and about possible changes you may make. The ancient wisdom of the goddesses gives support as well as provoking us to explore new ideas and challenges.

For your journey, you will need a large book in which you can write and draw your thoughts and feelings. Choose one with a lovely cover, which can become your special Goddess Book of Life. You will need pens and pencils and maybe crayons and felt-tip pens, and paints too if you wish. There are other simple materials you can acquire as you journey through the book. You may want to draw or note down your discoveries and reflections, and you probably will have new dreams to recount. Make your book into your own creative record of your experience, your thoughts and reflections – to help guide you through your lifestyle changes.

Sometimes your journey will be an adventure and there may be treasure at the end of the quest, but you may also need more quiet times when you wish to be still and reflect. Follow your inner guide and trust your intuition to create the right environment for this fresh beginning.

Maybe you are a person who races through a book and then goes back to read again at a slower pace; perhaps you are someone who reads a section at a time and gives it some thought before moving on. It is important that you read and reflect in your own unique way. There will be things that you go back to ponder in your own time anyway – you need to find your own rhythm and pace.

## BRINGING BALANCE TO LIFE

The philosophy that underpins this book is that the goddesses in their environment have an ancient wisdom that we need to remember: we need to reconnect with the old ways in a modern context in order to discover new pathways. Therefore, the goddesses are presented in their Elements, in their Heavenly Bodies or as symbols of the Journey of Life. Discovering the four elements will help us to bring balance to our lives. An appreciation of the stars, moon and sun reminds us of the magnificence of the celestial beings that also had very human attributes. And in our own personal journey of life we need symbols and rituals to assist us as we move on from difficult or unhelpful experiences and towards those that are supportive, creative and inspirational.

**Please note:** If you are receiving any kind of psychological treatment or medication, or are very stressed or vulnerable, you should consult your doctor or therapist before trying the exercises. Remember that many of the exercises can be tried out with a friend or a group.

*A*ncient goddesses, guide me on this journey, guide me to
stay still, guide me to see the signposts.

# SECTION 1

## AN INTRODUCTION TO THE ELEMENTS

The elements of Fire, Water, Earth and Air surround us in a myriad of ways; they help us to understand our environment and provide a context for living. All the elements exist in large forms such as raging forest fires and tempests and remind us that we cannot control nature, so we need to respect and care for our surroundings.

The elements are visible outside our homes in our gardens and parkland, woods and meadows, and we can experience them with all our senses. It is important for us to stay in touch with these sources from nature by experiencing them firsthand and not just through the television screen. We also bring the elements into our homes when we use candles, oil burners and log fires; house-plants and natural wood; water bowls and the gentle breeze blowing through wind chimes. And within our own body, our very breath is the air that is life-giving and energizing.

We may wear or carry with us symbols of the elements, and these are also important to help us stay in touch. Maybe we wear fiery colours, put on jewellery made with our birthstone, carry a vial of healing water or have a bird broach to remind us of soaring through the air – a symbol of freedom. When you have read this section, decide which element is most important for you now, and which goddess will help you to explore this element further.

*The* ELEMENTS *be kind to thee, and make thy* SPIRITS *all of comfort!*

*ANTHONY AND CLEOPATRA, 3.11.40*

# Fire

This SPARK will prove a raging fire,
If WIND and FUEL be brought to feed
it with.

HENRY VI, 3.11.302

Fire can be a positive energy: it lights our way, warms and dries us, cooks our food and flickers in the candle flame. We enjoy the natural flames of logs so much that we imitate them in gas fires if we have no fireplace. Fire also can be destructive and out of control: it can burn our houses, destroy forests and cause volcanic eruptions. Ancient fire rituals are almost always associated with women and goddesses. Fire rituals have survived since we first tamed fire to keep warm in the cave. The fireplace is the centre of many homes and candles are still lit at baptisms, at funerals and to celebrate birthdays. Fire rituals also exist for cleansing and purifying in traditional and modern medicine.

# GODDESSES & *Fire*

Fire has been associated with goddesses, female shamans and wise women since ancient times. Fire ceremonies have been performed to commemorate birth and death, to guard the hearth and light the way forward. Fire can glow peacefully or can be destructive. Fire can be used for celebration, for purification and for initiation.

The little chapel of the Burning Bush on Mount Sinai has an icon of the Virgin Mary with a burning thorn bush in her heart, and within the bush is Jesus, to whom she has given birth.

The fire and birth motif links us with Brigid (see page 20) and her midwife role. Fires are often lit at the time of birth in rural areas in Western Europe, Africa and Asia. Fire is also an aspect of Phosphoros, 'Bringing Light', who was associated with Artemis and childbirth, and is connected to Hecate, who carried a flaming torch.

Fire marked the initiation of the Inuit female shaman Uvavnuk, from the Arctic. Rasmussen (1927) says 'she had gone out to pass water. It was a dark winter evening, and suddenly a shining ball of fire showed in the sky. It came down to earth directly toward the place where Uvavnuk sat. She wanted to run away, but before she could do so, she was struck by the ball of fire. She became aware all at once that everything in her began to glow.'

The gate-keeping goddesses of ancient Egypt, goddesses of fire, also

Fuji, the fire goddess of Japan.

had an initiatory role. They guarded the gates of the underworld, and the dead had to name the goddesses before they were allowed to pass.

Many fire goddesses were thought to guard and protect at vulnerable times of change. They also looked after the house and the family. Fuji, the fire goddess from ancient Japan, was believed to be 'the ancestress and protectress' of the house; the extinct volcano Mount Fuji, Japan's sacred mountain, is named after her. The old goddess of the fire guards the fire in the centre of the house during the enactment of the bear sacrifice, which was performed by the Ainu peoples of the northern islands of Japan.

According to Gimbutas (1999), the Baltic peoples believed in Laima, the hearth-fire goddess who could also be a stork or a cockerel. The stork protects the house from thunderstorms and fires and safeguards the hearth for both the family and the community. The fire goddess is 'fed' when food is being cooked: bread and salt, or even a small loaf of bread, are offered to her.

The dancing gLu-maa Ghirdhima is a fire goddess from Tibet. Red in colour, she holds a lyre and is associated with music and song. Unusually, she is a peaceful fire goddess, and a Bodhisattva, one who will become a Buddha. The Tibetans consider her to be one of the eight mothers of Buddhism.

Fire as destroyer is associated with lightning and volcanoes and is typified by the goddess Pele, who rides her flaming chariot into the crater of Kilauea, in Hawaii.

The Haida of North America also have a volcano goddess: called Dzelarhons, she protects wild creatures and punishes people who kill them gratuitously.

The energy of the fire goddesses can connect us to our passion and sexuality, to clarity of thought and communication, to the creative and divine spark, and to the dancing joy for which we search in difficult times. In modern times fire is generally tamed but it can still get out of control. The goddesses remind us not to neglect fire, and to treat all fire with respect.

# Pele

Pele is the Hawaiian goddess of the volcano. She rides her chariot into the crater, sometimes in vengeance and sometimes in delight. Pele can be a wise old hag or a beautiful woman. She is one of the few goddesses whom the Hawaiians still venerate; they offer her white flowers or money.

Pele is a volatile goddess: sometimes she has all her fire under control as she sleeps peacefully, at other times she erupts uncontrollably. She was the daughter of the earth goddess Haumea and during her girlhood was fascinated by fires. This angered the sea goddess Namaka and there are stories of their conflicts, especially after Pele played with underground fires and caused large blazes to break out. Pele's mother decided that she should find a home of her own, so she set off with her sisters to create a new land. She created the Hawaiian islands by causing the volcanoes under the sea to have huge eruptions.

Pele was followed to Hawaii by Namaka and there was a furious fight between them, which ended in Pele transforming into steam and then leaping into the volcano. The Hawaiians deny that there has been human sacrifice to Pele, but until recently they have thrown hibiscus flowers, money, white birds and human hair into the crater.

Pele's volcano is Kilauea. The flaming crater is the highest point in the journey to the afterlife, where dangerous games are played in the leaping fire. There is no pain, only sheer delight and exhilaration. Pele is said to be seen by visitors to Hawaiian volcanoes as 'a wizened old woman who asks for a cigarette, lights it with a snap of her fingers, then disappears. Others say a red-robed woman dances on the rim of the fiery mountains.' (MONAGHAN 2000)

Pele's energy can be an inspiration to us because it helps us understand our outbursts of rage and know that they will calm. Pele shows us that volatile energy is important, life-giving and creative, but it needs to have focus. We too can sleep with our flames and not be consumed by them.

## A PELE DANCE OF LIFE AND INSPIRATION

Light a candle and place it safely. Choose your favourite rhythmic music. Close your eyes and visualize the candle flame. Allow the fire to enter your limbs slowly until you feel a surge of warmth. Slowly start to move to your music, until you are dancing in the flames. When you are ready to stop, gradually slow down. See the candle flame again in your mind's eye. Open your eyes and be aware of your new energy. Find others to share your dance of life and create your own 'dance of the flames'.

# Vesta, Sekhmet & Uvavnuk

## VESTA

Vesta is a virgin goddess of fire, one of the twelve great Roman divinities. Vesta's is the most important of the hearth cults that were practised, especially by royalty (her Greek counterpart is Hestia). In ancient times the hearth was considered

sacred and symbolized the 'centre of the house'. This circular hearth represents the original altar, an essentially female symbol, where food was cooked, sacrifices were made, prayers were offered, and the family or society gathered as a community. It was the place of warmth, where stories were told and songs were sung, and oral history passed from one generation to the next.

### A SYMBOL OF FIRE

Vesta was not represented by a statue or picture – she was the fire and the fire was her. She is perhaps less well-known now than other Roman goddesses because there were no images of her. When she did eventually appear on Roman coins she wore a mysterious veil, so that in ancient times her portrait was not defined. More than anything else she was a symbol, represented by fire, of the Roman society itself. This is why meticulous attention was paid to her shrine by the Vestal Virgins: if the fire was extinguished, it would mean the end of Roman society.

Vesta was worshipped daily at mealtimes in every household and in the temple in the Roman forum. Her sacred fire was believed to be the mystical beating of the heart of the city. It was tended continuously by the Vestal Virgins, who were chosen from girls between five and ten years, and who served for at least five years but often much longer. They were chosen by the high priest, the only man involved in the Vesta cult, and were regarded as the 'essence of Rome'. They had to take water from the sacred Spring of Juturna, as they were forbidden to use piped water. Vestal Virgins were highly respected, unless they lost their virginity, when severe punishment ensued. Many of the Vestal Virgins remained virgins – 'although free to marry once they had discharged their religious duties, they rarely did so, either from a continued commitment to the temple or because it was considered an ill omen' (Husain 1997).

Vesta's sacred animal is the ass, because an ass was said to have defended an attack on her virginity by Priapos. Millstones and the asses that turned them were decorated with flowers on 1 March, her feast day. Her sacred fire was dowsed and re-lit, and the laurel tree above her hearth in the temple was renewed.

She is again celebrated on 9 June, the sacred day of Vestalis. Salt cakes were baked on Vesta's hearth by her attendants and given as offerings for the ensuing eight days, and 'matrons' offered food cooked on their own hearths, a ritual that involved both the maiden and the mother. At the end of the festival the temple was cleaned by the Virgins and all waste thrown into the River Tiber.

HEARTH AND HOME
Vesta's circular hearth has inspired many buildings and landscaped gardens up to the present time. It is easy to forget the importance of the hearth – the place where we cook and welcome travellers, where we rest and warm ourselves. We also create our hearth in the outdoor fire of charcoal where we cook and celebrate the great outdoors.

### A VESTA INSPIRATION FOR YOUR HOME
Vesta symbolizes order and precision, clarity and purity. Give yourself time to focus on your living space. Walk around it slowly and imagine your hearth as a circular space or as an arc; you can add candles to your hearth, especially if you do not have a real fire. You can create your 'hearth in a circle' with candles, red pottery, a fire picture or fiery-coloured flowers. Absorb the energy from your fire centre. New stories will come to you in this space.

Always stay in touch with the centre.

*Let me find my warrior self to use with justice and humanity.*

*Let me find strength to assist others as well as myself.*

## SEKHMET

Sekhmet is an Egyptian warrior goddess of fire and heat. She is known by many names – Mistress of the Gods, Lion Goddess, Goddess of War, Goddess of Vengeance, the Mighty One of Enchantments. Sekhmet is usually depicted with the head of a

lion, who wears the solar disc, which is sometimes circled by the spitting cobra. She is also represented as a lioness whose 'mane smoked with fire, her back had the colour of blood, her countenance glowed like the sun, her eyes shone with fire' (quoted in Neumann 1970). The lion, the sun and the cobra all represent concentrated energy, which can be either creative or destructive.

It was Sekhmet's sheer power that was revered, but sometimes it could miss its mark, with disastrous results. A myth relates how humanity had to be saved from Sekhmet's slaughter:

*The goddess could not be stopped from her slaughter of the human race. The gods, to save humanity, ordered the brewing of 7,000 jars of beer, to which was added a red powder so that it represented human blood, then this liquid was poured out over the fields. With the coming of morning the goddess gazed at her reflection in it, drank it all and returned to her palace intoxicated. So it was that humanity was saved.*

(BARING AND CASHFORD, 1993)

There are several versions of this story, for example the red was made from pomegranate juice, or wine was used rather than beer, but the essential core meaning is the same – rage can be energy that is misdirected.

Sekhmet was invoked by the Egyptians because her warlike force could overcome their enemies. And the above story shows how war energy can temporarily get out of control, before it is restored to an equilibrium. This energy is not always destructive and there are stories, for example, of surges of maternal energy in order to protect children. It is when this energy is misplaced that it becomes destructive, and assistance is needed to create a balance.

Sekhmet's dynamic energy was also focused on overcoming disease, and she was called upon by her followers for healing. She could cleanse the world of evil and pollution and make it a better place for future generations. She was also believed to care for the human body in the underworld.

Sekhmet's gentler side is sometimes conflated into Bast, the cat goddess whom we shall meet later (see page 158). However, both these goddesses are connected with the deities Ra and Hathor (see page 136) and are also believed to have healing aspects.

## UVAVNUK

Uvavnuk, a female shaman of the Inuit peoples, gives us a quite different focus that is influenced by fire. We have already heard how she conquered her fear when struck by the lightning bolt, and she then discovered that whenever she was frightened, singing would turn her fear to joy:

*As soon as she began to sing, she became delirious with joy, and all the others in the house were beyond themselves with joy, because their* minds were being cleansed of all that burdened them. They lifted up their arms and cast away everything connected with suspicion and malice.

(RASMUSSEN, 1927)

The following chant and dance is inspired by the fire goddesses and will give you a focus for developing and containing your fire energy, either as an individual or with a group of your friends, 'the fire people'. You may wish to add more lines to the chant and make it truly your own.

## A FIRE CHANT AND DANCE

PELE, SEKHMET, VESTA, UVAVNUK
PELE, SEKHMET, VESTA, UVAVNUK

*Give me some wildness
Contain my rage
Transform my energy
into action*

*Challenge my inertia
Inspire new directions
Let me protect the vulnerable*

PELE, SEKHMET, VESTA, UVAVNUK
PELE, SEKHMET, VESTA, UVAVNUK

# Brigid

Brigid is the patron of midwives and fugitives, blacksmiths and poets, fertility and healing, corn and cattle. She is known by many names: The Bright One, Lady of the Shores, Brigid of the Green Mantle, Bright Arrow, The High One, and Sacred Midwife and Healer.

Countless stories are told about Brigid. Goddess, saint and deity, Brigid is known in many forms and in many cultures. She loved animals and is said to have been the midwife at the birth of Christ. According to myth, she hung her wet robe on a ray of the sun to dry.

Brigid is thought to be a Celtic goddess who was incorporated into the sixth century saint, Brigid of Kildare, Ireland, and Bride in Scotland. She is also linked with Brig, goddess of

BRIGID FEED ME FOR THE COMING YEAR
BRIGID INSPIRE FOR THE COMING YEAR
BRIGID BLESS THOSE AROUND ME

high places, war, water and well-being, who inspired the Brigantes, an ancient culture in north England (from where we get the word brigand).

Brigid is a fire goddess who is blessed by heavenly flames. She lights the fires in the hearths of poor people, just as her followers keep continuous lamps alight at her shrine. Brigid's fire warms us and lights our way, and she kindles the light inside us to sustain us through difficult times.

Brigid is revered on 1 February, the Celtic first day of Spring, the feast of Imbolc. The land is about to grow again after the waiting of winter and we see the first lambs and the snowdrops. We can cleanse our homes with burning sage as a fire ritual of purification as we prepare for Imbolc. It is a time for special celebrations with family and friends, which can include seasonal baking, log fires and storytelling.

Brigid is associated with sheep and cows and with milk; she is said to have been bathed in milk when she was born. Brigid the mother can remind us that we can mother ourselves if we feel neglected, giving ourselves the nurturing we feel we need.

## A BRIGID RITUAL FOR HOPE AND INSPIRATION

Choose some time for yourself in a quiet, perfumed space. Select a new white candle and holder and sit comfortably as you meditate on the flame. Slowly close your eyes and allow the flame to connect with your inner flame, your fiery strength, your inspiration from Brigid. Slowly open your eyes, breathe softly the perfumed air, and feel blessed for the coming year.

# FIRE GODDESS *Stories* & EXERCISES

The fire goddesses come to us in many aspects – wise old crone, nurturing matron, warrior woman and beautiful maiden. They present us with many different aspects of the energy of fire, and we are constantly reminded that both our inner fire and the fire outside can either create inspiration and comfort or rage and get out of control.

## BRIGID'S STORY

The fire goddess Brigid was associated with the ritual fires for purification in ancient times. The Christian transformation to St Brigid placed her at the head of a women's holy group that maintained her sacred fire, the monastic hearth, every day of the year. Brigid's fire was extinguished during the Norman invasion of Ireland in 1220, and then rekindled and kept alight until the Reformation and dissolution of the monasteries in the sixteenth century.

It has been suggested that the origins of Brigid or Bride date back to pre-Celtic times. Stories relate that the Cailleach, an old hag of Wales, kept a maiden called Bride imprisoned on the top of Ben Nevis. Her son fell in love with Brigid, and he freed her and they ran away together. The old woman pursued them across many lands and caused terrible storms, but she was turned into stone and Brigid was freed. Bride then became the goddess venerated in spring and summer.

Brigid can inspire us in many ways; this story can show us the many perceptions and transformations of Brigid. We can keep her fire alight for ourselves and for others and find freedom from the ties that stop us achieving what we desire in life. We can mark the turning of the seasons with our own fire rituals with family and friends. Fire may also help us to overcome our difficulties if we listen to our fire-self, our inner fire, and explore the element of fire through symbols.

## THE FIRE MASK

This exercise will help you to contact your own inner fire. You will need a large piece of drawing paper and crayons or felt-tipped pens in strong colours. Sit in a comfortable space, on a cushion or in a chair, and close your eyes. Breathe evenly for a few moments and imagine you are staring into a large fire with dancing flames. Allow your imagination

## A NURTURING EXERCISE

Brigid can help us look after ourselves. Brigid the mother reminds us that we can mother ourselves if we feel neglected. For example, you can heat a mug of whichever milk you can drink (cow, sheep, goat, rice or soya), stir in some honey, sprinkle with cinnamon and drink it slowly. Feel nurtured as you drink.

to wander through the fire, following all the different shapes and movements. Maybe you can see landscapes, or animals or little people. Allow yourself to look for a face or faces in the flames — you may have to be patient. Let the fire give you the gift of a mask. Open your eyes slowly and create the mask with your drawing materials. Explore this mask of fire energy and reflect on this gift and how it may help you on your journey.

## SEKHMET MEDITATIONS

Sit quietly by a fire or candle, breathing gently in and out to find a calm rhythm. If you have low energy and have ruled out all medical causes, reflect on the fiery energy of Sekhmet. Picture her riding her lion in the brilliant sun, and allow the warmth to enter your being. Make a choice to do something physical and energetic.

If you are someone who overflows with energy, breathe gently to start the meditation and acknowledge to

yourself how difficult it is to sit still. Ask yourself whether your energy spills over in an unfocused way. For example, do you suddenly explode with anger that is out of proportion to what has happened? Or do you put more energy than is needed into a task so that there is no time for anything else? Reflect on the possibility of creating a rhythm of your energy. For example, instead of running round the block, try running the first stretch, walking the second stretch. Continue to alternate running and walking.

## A FIRE GIFT FOR YOU AND YOUR FRIENDS

Light a new fire of oak logs and place an iron cauldron or pot, half filled with spring water, on the flames. Stir in freshly picked herbs, such as sage, rosemary, thyme or mint, and allow the pot to simmer gently while you breathe in the pure aromatic steam that will pervade the air around you. Focus on the burning logs and allow yourself to calm your inner rage or to light your inner flame. Repeat the following invocation:

GODDESS OF FIRE — FIRE MY RESOLVE
GODDESS OF FIRE — FIRE MY RESOLVE

GODDESS OF FIRE — BURN UP MY RAGE
GODDESS OF FIRE — BURN UP MY RAGE

GODDESS OF FIRE — FIRE UP MY IMAGINATION
GODDESS OF FIRE — FIRE UP MY IMAGINATION

LET THERE BE PEACE IN MY HEART AND A
LIGHT ON MY PATH. LET ME GIVE THANKS

# Water

This MUSIC crept by me upon the WATERS.

*THE TEMPEST, I.II.391*

Water covered the earth before there was land, and humans evolved from that primeval water. Water is necessary for all fertility – of the land, the creatures and ourselves. We spend nine months in water in the womb, and we shed copious tears when we laugh or cry. Water allows us to feel supported, relaxed and in tune with ourselves and our surroundings. Water can trickle as a mountain stream or become a raging torrent: likewise the sound of water can be challenging or soothing. Still, deep water creates a mirror for our reflection. Water can wash away our troubles, help us to go with the flow and to find calm and relaxation.

# GODDESSES & *Water*

Water goddesses have always been guardians of springs, wells and rivers. Water rituals still take place for naming ceremonies, blessings, healing and consecration, and birth and death rituals. Water is significant at most rites of passage. Many healing wells are dedicated to goddesses; bathing in their waters is thought to bring about cures.

Oshun is a well-known water goddess of the Yoruba in Nigeria. Born at the headwaters of the Oshun river, she cures the sick and promotes fertility with her 'sweet waters'. Essentially a goddess of women, Oshun promotes childbirth and the continuation of the tribe. This story explains how, through her cunning, she learned divination:

*Oshun wanted to use shells for divination but Obatala [father of wisdom] would not teach her, so Oshun decided to use her cunning. Obatala was bathing one day in the river, and the trickster Elegba stole his 'white cloth'. Oshun told Obatala that she would find his white cloth if he agreed to show her divination; she gave him his cloth and he taught her divination.*

(ADAPTED FROM ANN AND IMEL, 1993)

The Temiar people of Malaysia believe that Old Mother Chengkai was their founding mother, shaman-midwife. She and her familiars danced and tranced their world into being. The Temiars live in houses built on stilts on the banks of rivers; the river orientates them in space. If they are taken away from the river, they become disoriented. Temiar midwives have a senior ritual status, like shamans, and these wise women are valued during dangerous times such as childbirth. The midwife uses warm water symbolically to cleanse the woman during rites of passage. At first menstruation, water is poured from on high over the young girl and she is then wrapped in a new sarong to celebrate her new status. After

childbirth, the mother is ritually bathed inside the house, then clothed in an old, clean sarong. For the Temiars it is vital that the water is warmed, that it has been through a process of change from its natural state to become a transformed cultural symbol.

Egle, known as Queen of the Serpents, is a Slavic and Lithuanian goddess of water, reptiles and families. Her story gives us a three-generation myth about separation and transformation. One day, when Egle was swimming, she found a serpent in her clothes, who wanted to marry her. After the wedding, when Egle returned to her husband's palace under the sea, he turned into a handsome prince. They lived happily and had four children. Then Egle took the children home to see their grandparents who, by trickery, discovered the secret name of the serpent from one of the children. They called him out of the sea and killed him. When Egle found out what had happened, she turned herself and the children into trees.

The Apsarases are Hindu celestial nymphs who give solace to deities and

Oshun, a water goddess of the Yoruba in Nigeria.

the souls of dead warriors. They are the essence of water. They symbolize clouds or mist: the nurturing qualities of water. They can change into water birds. One of them, Adrika, was changed into a fish. She gave birth to a son and a daughter; the spell was broken and she was taken to heaven.

The water goddesses give us gifts of energy, transformation and nurture. They remind us to find our flow in life and to mark our life stages with rituals. Life is too complex to be understood all at once; we need to be able to step onto the banks of the river of life and take stock. Water rituals are markers of transitions, and affirm our identity in our new status.

# Isis

Isis, the Egyptian Goddess who is associated with water and ships, is also known as Queen of the Earth, The Moon, Goddess of Life and Healing, Protectress of the Dead, Mother of the Seasons, and Queen of the Stars. Isis is known for her magic and healing powers and for her gifts to women.

Isis journeys in a moon boat with Ra the sun god, as he travels from the West to rise again in the East. Some illustrations of moon boats show the protective eye of Horus, who was born of Isis and Osiris after she breathed life back into Osiris. When the soul leaves the body it 'breathes the breath of Isis'; it is given the first breath of eternal life as Isis beats her wings.

> MAY THE MOISTURE BEGIN TO
> MOUNT FOR THIS SPIRIT!
> MAY THE CANALS BE FILLED
> THROUGH YOU!
> MAY THE NAMES OF THE RIVERS BE
> CREATED THROUGH YOU!
> OSIRIS, LIVE!
> OSIRIS, LET THE GREAT LISTLESS
> ONE ARISE!
>
> I am Isis
> (QUOTED IN RUNDLE CLARK, 1978)

Isis sometimes appears as a bird: as a swallow when looking for her murdered husband Osiris, and as a kite when she beat her wings to bring him back to life. When she put his dismembered body back together and bound him, she became the first person to practise embalming. Her all-enveloping wings protect her husband, her son and all her people.

Isis is still associated with the River Nile. Egyptian creation stories describe the primeval waters from which the first hill emerged, followed by islands that became populated with animals and people. Every year the Nile evaporates into the earth, then flows more and more strongly until it floods, mirroring the primeval waters. As the flood-waters, the tears of Isis, subside, the 'pregnant earth' begins to grow crops. Isis taught women to spin flax, grind corn and weave cloth and how to tame men so they can live together.

## AN ISIS EXERCISE FOR RELAXATION AND CALM

Take a large piece of paper and crayons. Half fill a special bowl with water. Sit quietly and close your eyes. Move your head from side to side, and breathe gently to remove any tension. Open your eyes and raise your arms; allow them to move in relaxed, rhythmic wave shapes. Now trickle the water in the bowl through your fingers and listen to the sounds. Finally, draw patterns of flowing water, ripples and waves, in different colours. Sit and think about the gentle waves you have made.

# Epona, Cordelia & Yemaya

## EPONA

Epona, the Celtic horse goddess, has ancient associations with water, and is thought to have been a spring or river goddess. One of her manifestations is as a fast-flowing river and many of her shrines have been found near healing springs. As flowing water she was associated with fertility and abundance, and she was also invoked at times of illness.

Water and horses are associated in many different cultures. We talk about foaming waves as 'white horses' and in France a rough sea is the 'white mare'. In Germany there is a mythical horse who paws the ground with his foot to make a new spring flow across the land.

Epona's father apparently hated women, so he mated with a mare who gave birth to a beautiful girl. The mare was thought to be a divine horse because she could speak to her daughter and gave her the name of Epona. Epona could take the form of a horse or a human, although the horse is usually considered her totem. She is usually depicted riding her horse, either astride or side-saddle – occasionally she is seen lying naked across the horse's back.

Epona protects domestic animals such as cows, horses and asses as well as wild birds. The flock of birds also associates her with 'The Happy Otherworld'. She was adopted by the Romans to protect their horses

### EPONA MEDITATION FOR STRENGTH AND FREEDOM

This exercise is ideally undertaken outdoors, especially on a windy day. As you go walking, think about Epona's large white mare. Picture her in the landscape and see Epona, beautifully attired, climb on her back and start to canter over the land. She jumps across the fast-flowing river and heads towards the sea, then comes to a stop on the sea shore. Epona and her horse stand on the sand and look out to sea. The waves come in to shore gently and then build up and up to huge proportions. The white mane of the sea tosses as the waves grow bigger, and horse and rider feel the tang of the sea spray. They stand quite still, communing with the spirit of deep water. As the waves subside, Epona and her white horse give blessing and then trot out of sight. Reflect on your feelings during the visualization, and on your own relationship with the water and the landscape. Write a poem or a story about this experience.

and many little statues of her have been found across Europe in stables and outbuildings. She is the only non-Roman goddess to be honoured by the Romans under her own name. They built a shrine to her at the barracks of the Imperial bodyguard and garlanded her with roses.

### EPONA'S SYMBOLS

Epona is thought to have been invoked at some royal unions in Celtic times, when the king symbolically married a white mare. Recent archaeological research suggests that the White Horse at Uffington, England, a horse carved into the white chalk hillside, is much more ancient than at first thought, and that it is likely to be a giant representation of Epona. Standing in the eye of the carved horse is supposed to bring good fortune.

The symbols of Epona are a key, a whip, a sheaf of corn, a goblet, a cornucopia and a sun disk, although the latter two may have been added later by the Romans.

## CORDELIA

Cordelia was originally a Celtic sea goddess, daughter of the sea god Llyr. She later became known for her associations with spring and summer flowers. She is honoured at the Celtic festival of Beltane, on 1 May, when the cattle herds are turned out into the meadows for the summer. Beltane is an ancient fertility ritual that is also associated with the Green Man and maypoles. The festival is supposed to attract witches and fairies, so whatever mischief has been happening in the woods, people are advised not to sleep out of doors.

> OH DO NOT TELL THE
> PRIEST OUR PLIGHT,
> OR HE WILL CALL IT A SIN;
> BUT — WE HAVE BEEN OUT IN
> THE WOODS ALL NIGHT,
> A-CONJURING SUMMER IN!
>
> (KIPLING, 'A TREE SONG', 1913)

Cordelia appears at Beltane, while the god of air and the god of the underworld fight over her. This ritual is still enacted in some parts of Europe. Symbolically, we can see that the spirit above the earth and the spirit under the earth fight over the water spirit that is on the earth. Cordelia is, of course, re-created as the youngest daughter of King Lear in Shakespeare's play. The play is based on 'nature' and there are many references to the goddess as well as to natural and unnatural behaviour. There are curses

*Goddess of the flowing waters cleanse me for my journey, refresh me when I am weary, calm me from my fears.*

directed at nature to blight fertility as well as rituals to promote fertility, both of the land and the daughters. It can be read as a Celtic myth about a god-king who is abdicating and moving towards his own death. Throughout the story there are images of water, including tears, storms, rain, hurricanes, raging seas and rivers. Cordelia's story helps us to get in touch with ambivalent feelings we may have about our fathers, especially when they become crazy in old age, as Cordelia's father does in the play. It helps us to explore issues of both dependence and independence, as Cordelia eventually makes her own decisions. If you do not know this story, watch one of the videos or see *King Lear* at the theatre.

## YEMAYA

Yemaya is an African Goddess of the ocean whose following later spread to the West Indies and Brazil as well as to parts of Europe, where she is known by many names. She is considered to be the mother of waters, Mama Watta, who gave birth to all the world's waters, even in her sleep. In her homeland in Nigeria, the Yoruba people say she is the goddess of the Ogun river, the daughter of the sea, into which she constantly empties herself.

Yemaya is often depicted as emerging from the sea, covered in shells. She is a goddess of the senses, feelings and inevitability. She represents love between friends and partners and between parents and children. There is a simplicity and straight-forwardness in her love on the one hand, and the unstoppable might of the sea on the other.

Yemaya is an ocean goddess of the crescent moon in the Macumba cult, and crowds gather on the beaches of Bahia in Brazil to honour her feast day on 2 February. Letters of request to Yemaya are thrown into the sea and she is offered sweet gifts – precious stones, perfume and fabrics.

Yemaya has the colours blue-turquoise and white, and her followers wear necklaces of seven blue beads alternating with seven crystals. Yemaya's symbols are seashells, a gourd rattle, an anchor, a key and turquoise.

## YEMAYA'S GIFT

Decide on a corner of your house or garden where you can create shapes and patterns. Take time out at the seaside to collect special shells, stones, pieces of driftwood and other treasures. You may find pieces of coloured glass that remind you of Yemaya's stones. You may choose to make a bed of sand for your collection. Create circles and spirals, lines and zig-zags – any patterns that give you pleasure. Find different ways of grouping them. Enjoy the process of creating your pictures and leave them for meditation. They can be changed and added to later.

# Sedna

Sedna is the Arctic sea goddess of the Inuit people. She is queen of all sea-creatures and lives at the bottom of the sea. Although she started life as a beautiful young woman, she was later transformed, becoming half-woman, half-fish, with the ability to change into either.

Associated with wild birds, heaven and hell, and beauty, Sedna is concerned with the welfare of her creatures, and guards hunting methods. If hunters use traditional methods, she will allow a number of the animals to be captured. Today she is considered an upholder of conservation of the environment. However, if the hunters do not use the old ways, she disrupts their hunting with violent storms and a shaman has to visit her and intercede.

### SEDNA'S STORY
Sedna refused all suitors who wanted to marry her until one day a stranger arrived, cloaked in sealskins. She went with him and he removed his cloak; he was the stormy petrel sea-bird. He took her to his nest, which was filthy, and Sedna wanted to return home. Her father came to rescue her in his kayak, but the bird followed them and a storm approached. As a sacrifice to calm the water, her father threw Sedna out of the boat; she clung desperately to the side. Her father chopped off her fingers, and still she clung on. He chopped her fingers three times and eventually she had to let go and sank to the bottom of the sea. The pieces of her hands became different sea creatures and Sedna now rules the bottom of the sea. She guards over heaven and hell. If the hunters are unable to hunt, one of the shamans must visit her, but it is very perilous and he has to pass through dangerous obstacles – dead souls, the ice wheel, a cauldron and a fierce dog. He then has to comb the seaweed out of her hair, because she has no hands. Then, and only, then will Sedna grant the request.

Sedna is similar to mermaids and silkies, half-human, half-fish creatures who lure fishermen to their deaths. They also can be compared to the sirens of ancient Greece.

### SEDNA'S STORY FOR US
Next time you have a meal of fish, think about Sedna's story and her estrangement from her father. Could we forgive such aggression and selfishness? Perhaps we still carry a burden of guilt for cruel things we have done to others. If we can learn to forgive ourselves, we may also learn to forgive other people. After this contemplation, invoke Sedna to carry away your guilt and sadness on her waves. Eat the meal as a ritual to Sedna.

# WATER GODDESS *Stories* & EXERCISES

The water goddesses give us wisdom in times of stress and grief or when we are in need of comfort and support. If we find ourselves at a crossroads, they can help us flow in the right direction, and if we feel we are drowning, they can remind us that the water supports us; we do not need to go under. And if we are treading water, we can look at the landscape and take joy in the waiting.

### ISIS' STORY OF GRIEF AND HOPE

Isis was married to Osiris, who was killed by his jealous brother Set. Set had built an ornate chest and he said whoever it fitted could have it as a gift. Osiris lay in it and Set nailed the lid down and set it adrift in the sea. The chest washed up on the shores of Byblus, where it grew into a tamarisk tree. The king of Byblus cut it down and used it as a pillar when building his palace.

When Isis discovered what had happened, she was distraught and cut off her hair and tore her clothes in her grief. She set out on a long search for her beloved, calling and crying for him. She came to the king's palace and took a job as a nursemaid, looking after the baby prince. Isis changed into a swallow and fluttered around the pillar that contained Osiris, desperate to find him. Since she had goddess powers she decided to give the gift of immortality to the young prince in her care, so she wrapped him in swaddling clothes and placed him in the fire. The queen snatched the baby, fearing the worst, and Isis had to disclose her true identity. The queen then gave Isis the tamarisk tree containing Osiris' body.

When Set learned what had happened, he stole the body and chopped it up into many pieces and scattered it across the land. Isis found every piece apart from his penis and so she fashioned one out of pure gold. Isis breathed Osiris' body back together again. She changed into a kite and, beating her wings, she breathed life into him once more, and they conceived their son Horus.

### HEALING LOSS

Isis can be a comfort to us when life seems dark. We can gain inspiration from her energy and determination to find Osiris. We can understand her tears at the loss of her beloved. We can fly with her as

### WATER SONGS AND CHANTS

You probably already know many songs that have derived from water – 'The Skye Boat Song', 'Row, Row, Row the Boat' or 'Moon River', not to mention sea shanties and pirate songs of all descriptions! The young girls in Malaysia cup their hands to make music in the water and hum while they are doing it. Try doing the same in a bowl or in your bath.

the swallow in her search and celebrate in the finding of the tamarisk tree. We can see her as the kite who generates life-giving breath from her wings.

Look at the illustration of Isis with wings (opposite) or find a picture of a kite or an owl with outspread wings and use the picture for a meditation exercise. Imagine yourself able to fly with outstretched wings across the landscape. There you can see those you have lost, people in your life or aspects of your own life or things that were special to you. Acknowledge each one of them as important in their own way, but now it is time to let go of them. It is time to be free. In your mind's eye bring together all these losses and place them in a boat shaped like a crescent moon. Allow your wings to beat a gentle breeze that lets the boat sail safely towards the horizon. Now turn your wings to envelop and protect yourself at this vulnerable time. Imagine you are encircled in the wings of Isis and feel safe and loved.

## WATER IN THE GARDEN

Even the smallest garden can have a water feature; in a tiny courtyard you can place a spout on the wall and create a wonderful soothing sound. Waterfalls, springs and fountains will both attract wildlife and create a special space where you can be with yourself. Choose your water source with care so that it is unique to you: it might be a lion's head, a nymph, a wolf howling, a series of lipped bowls, a green man or a goddess urn. Let it express you in your surroundings.

## WATER IN THE HOME

Is your bathroom a functional place you dash in and out of or is it a place where you can relax and reflect? Find ways to make it more soothing and pleasurable. Try bathing by candlelight, using sweet-smelling soaps and thick warm towels. Have water pictures on the ceiling that you can look at, or sea tiles on the shower walls. Try to make curves by using shells and soft curtains to soften sharp edges. Experience the power of water to heal and purify and to cleanse and renew.

THANKS BE TO THE MIGHTY SEAS
THANKS BE TO THE FLOWING RIVERS
THANKS BE TO THE TINY STREAM
THANKS BE TO THE HEALING SPRING
THANKS BE TO THE PUDDLE IN MY PATH
THANKS BE

# Earth

Earth is a vital
element for security
and growth. Earth is actually with us,
under our feet, the whole time. We
speak of being 'on firm ground' or
'putting down roots', and we kiss the
earth when we return to our homeland.
Earth gives us food, shelter and the
beauty of nature. We can dance on the
earth in celebration and thanksgiving.
Most of us like to have a garden that we
can care for, and take delight in growing
plants to eat or to attract birds or
tending flowers for pleasure; this little
piece of nature brings us closer to the
earth. Most of the ancient earth rituals
are associated with women – the earth-
mother goddesses in their many forms.

Then must thou needs
find out new HEAVEN and
new EARTH.

*ANTHONY AND CLEOPATRA, 1.1.17*

# GODDESSES & *Earth*

Mother Earth herself is one of the ancient 'great' goddesses of the natural world, and the container of all water. Trees, with their roots deep in the soil and their branches reaching for the sky, often symbolize earth.

The Tree of Life in its many forms is seen as the connection between the earth and the heavens, and can be seen continuing as the Cross of Jesus.

Earth rites are especially important for agriculturalists and cultivators, and

### A FRUITFUL THOUGHT

Give yourself some time in your garden, the park or at your window. Choose your favourite fruit with skin and sit with your eyes closed. Feel the texture of the skin, any bumps or stalks, any irregularities in shape. Smell the fruit and connect with any pleasurable memories it evokes. Open your eyes and gaze on your fruit, seeing it afresh after touching and smelling it. Now slowly eat it as if tasting it for the first time. Give thanks to the earth for the fruit.

many cultures have their own different fertility goddesses. Many rituals are associated with the planting and harvesting of crops. For example, in Romania the farmer will place a loaf of bread in the first furrow, to ensure a plentiful crop; in other countries, milk is poured into the first furrow. In many Asian countries, at planting time some rice grains are reserved for the following year, either to sprinkle on the ground or to mix with the new seed, like a 'fertility of continuity'. Grain is also thrown at weddings to ensure fertility – an echo of ancient rites to acknowledge the earth goddesses.

The bog goddess of Ireland is an earth goddess of the peat beds: the bog itself is believed to be the goddess. The goddess nourishes the earth, providing healing herbs and fuel for winter. It is possible that in ancient times she demanded human sacrifice.

A Native American interviewed by Eliade (1959) describes his poignant feeling about violating the earth when he is asked to plough:

*Shall I take a knife and tear my
mother's bosom?
Then when I die she will not take me
to her bosom to rest.
You ask me to dig for stone! Shall I dig
under her skin for bones?
Then when I die, I cannot enter her
body to be born again.*

The Greek goddess Gaia, known as the 'deep-breasted', was believed to have given birth to the whole world, to the gods and to humans. The sky god Uranus and the sea god Pontus were two of her sons; Gaia went on to give birth to the Titans, the Cyclops and several monsters through her union with Uranus. He was so appalled at his offspring that he shut them away deep in the earth. Gaia was so angry that she persuaded the youngest Titan, Cronus, to castrate Uranus and where his blood dropped on the earth, there grew the giants and the tree nymphs, the Erinyes and the Meliae. There are many other potent myths across cultures, of blood and earth creating new beings. There is also the opposite situation, of human or animal blood contaminating the land, especially after wars, and cleansing of the earth being necessary to remove the pollution.

Whereas the Roman goddess Flora is associated with flowers and spring, Pomona is the goddess of fruit trees and marks the harvest in the autumn. Her sacred grove, Pomonal, was on the road from Rome to Ostia. Pomona is especially associated with apples, eaten as a sacred fruit by the Romans, and is linked with the Isle of Avalon.

The Song of Solomon in the Old Testament creates images of love and heightened sexual union through metaphors of earth and nature:

*I am the rose of Sharon and the
lily of the valleys.
As the lily among thorns, so is my love
among the daughters.
As the apple tree among the trees
of the wood, so is my beloved
among the sons.*

Pomona, Roman goddess of fruit trees and the harvest.

# Asherah

Asherah, the oldest of the Canaanite goddesses, is also known as Mother Goddess, Giver of Life, Mistress of Sexual Rejoicing, Creatress of the Gods, Creatress of all Animals and Lady Who Traverses the Sea. She is said to have given birth to seventy gods, including Baal, Mot and Anath.

Asherah is always associated with trees, and many of her pictures depict her as the Tree of Life. Her images have been found in temples, on hill tops, and in sacred groves. She is often represented by carved or plain pieces of wood, named *asherim*, or by the sycamore, fig or mulberry tree.

Asherah figurines have fulsome breasts, with her hands cupped beneath them, suggesting nurture and plenty. Her lower body is not defined, but is a long robe, that possibly stood in or on the earth. She is described as riding a sacred lion, naked and with lilies and serpents in upraised hands.

Asherah is mentioned at least forty times in the Old Testament and is named in the Book of Joshua as one of the false gods against whom the Hebrews waged war when they invaded Canaan. Canaan was the 'promised land', and the Hebrews found a fertile land with a thriving goddess religion. The destruction of the *asherim* and the goddess beliefs was not always successful, and aspects of Asherah's cult were imported, even into the Temple of Jerusalem. Subsequent kings tried alternately to destroy and then restore her for many hundreds of years, and when the people of Judah were exiled into Egypt, the prophet Jeremiah blamed their worship of false idols. The people spoke back and said their troubles had started when they stopped giving offerings to their goddesses.

Asherah reminds us of the strength and rootedness that can never be destroyed or taken away from us. We can reflect on her sacred groves, her rich and abundant mulberry trees with burgeoning fruit, running with thick red juice. If we feel unsteady, rootless or unsure of where to place ourselves, we can be inspired by the solid earth that is Asherah's and by her Tree of Life.

## TREE OF LIFE EXERCISE INSPIRED BY ASHERAH

Wherever you are standing, place your feet the same width apart as your shoulders. Close your eyes and imagine your feet have strong roots that penetrate deep into the earth. Feel sap coming up through your roots and into your feet, until it flows through your whole body. The energy of the earth allows you to grow upwards and outwards. Blessed be Asherah.

# Black Madonna, Our Lady of Guadalupe

### THE BLACK MADONNA

The Black Madonna or Black Virgin presents us with one of the most intriguing mysteries in goddess work. Black representations of Mary have emerged in North Africa, Europe, the Americas and Asia. Some clergy deny the existence of Black Madonnas and explain them away as smoke-damaged, or a product of dark-skinned people making them in their own image, or people mistakenly imagining that she would be dark simply because she comes from a hot climate.

'I am Black but I am Beautiful, O ye daughters of Jerusalem' is sung in The Song of Songs, which contains some of the most beautiful sexual imagery written about women and their lovers. 'I am Black but I am Beautiful' is an important and positive role model for black women. Who is the Dark Lady of the Old Testament? We ask the same question of the Dark Lady of Shakespeare's sonnets.

### FERTILITY GODDESSES

Black Madonnas occur too widely to be dismissed with simplistic explanations. The general opinion is that they have their roots in the ancient beliefs concerning earth and fertility goddesses, that they became incorporated into the mythology of Isis, Cybele and Minerva, and were again transformed and integrated into Christianity. New Black Madonnas have been seen in visions in more recent times, such as Our Lady of Guadalupe (see page 46).

Figurines of black goddesses have been found when ploughing fields, indicating the links with the earth

*Black goddess of mystery, remind me*
*of who I am and where I am going and*
*help me to keep my vision.*

# & Pachamama

mother goddesses of fertility. Black stone statues depict Isis with Horus on her lap, and Isis suckling her child. Medieval statues of the Black Madonna are found in Catholic countries such as France and Spain, as are wooden figurines carved from olive, oak or fruit trees. The Crusaders brought some of these back from the Holy Land and placed them in shrines rededicated to Mary.

In the early Middle Ages, shrines to the Black Virgin were popular sites for veneration and pilgrimage. They were found in churches, crypts, caves, sacred groves or wells, some of which belonged to the older goddess mythology of Isis, Cybele and Minerva. With the coming of Christianity these sites were rededicated to the Virgin Mary. Black Virgins appear at various sites in France and some are named after trees: Our Lady of the Hollies, Our Lady of the Thornbush, Our Lady of the Dark Forest, Our Lady of the Brambles and Our Lady of the Oak Tree all connect Mary both with the ancient nature shrines and also with sacred groves and the ancient goddess.

## VENERATING BLACK MADONNA

The cult of Black Madonnas proliferated during the ninth and tenth centuries. A small figure called the Madonna of Monserrat, Spain, was discovered by shepherds in a cave, where she had been hidden during the Moorish wars. Royalty and ordinary people alike gave gifts, and sometimes great riches. The statues were adorned with fine clothes and jewels, and some were placed on the popular pilgrimage route to Santiago de Compostela in northern Spain.

St Bernard of Clairvaux is said as a boy to have received three drops of milk from the breast of the Black Virgin of Chatillon, which was claimed to be the inspiration that led him to create a thriving chain of abbeys and the monastic order of the Cistercians across Western and Eastern Europe. He wrote many sermons on the theme of the Song of Songs, Solomon and the Queen of Sheba. He also encouraged the pilgrimage to Compostela, which is sometimes called the Milky Way. People still walk this inspiring pilgrimage.

THE CULT OF THE BLACK MADONNA
Whatever our beliefs, the Black Virgin or Black Madonna is shrouded in mystery and at times secrecy. Many of her statues have been stolen, others are locked away and even researchers are denied access. It is thought that there may be a Black Madonna cult even now, which has survived from Crusader times. Which of the several Marys is the Black Madonna? Mary the Virgin, Mary Magdalene or Mary the Egyptian? Or is she indeed Sara, beloved of gypsies, a black Egyptian servant whom some believed would give birth to the cult of Black Virgins? So much is guesswork and some, indeed, romanticism. However, we do know that the links between the Black Virgin or Madonna, the mother goddesses of Greece, Rome and Egypt and the ancient earth goddess beliefs create lines back to our most primitive past.

Black Madonnas are associated with miracles; in particular, they are believed to be able to resuscitate dead babies in order for them to be baptized. They are called upon to ease childbirth and to make women fertile. Images of nature, sexuality and fertility are expressed through ritual, song and poetry, for the earth and for lovers.

OUR LADY OF GUADALUPE
Whereas most of the Black Madonnas discussed have African and European roots, Our Lady of Guadalupe is of sixteenth-century Amerindian origin. She manifested herself to a Mexican farmer after a burst of birdsong, when he had a vision of a beautiful black woman in fine clothes, surrounded by jewels and gold, who was 'shining like the sun'. The site of his vision was an ancient Aztec shrine, probably the site of the serpent goddess Coatlicue. He persuaded the Church authorities that his vision was indeed of the Virgin Mary, and she is now Queen and patron saint of Mexico. Our Lady of Guadalupe is venerated on 12 December, and is another variation on the Black Madonna stories.

The Black Madonna keeps us in touch with life's mysteries, especially

*Pachamama keep my feet on the ground and let me see again the fruitful harvest and your gifts of plenty.*

the mysteries of the earth, of sexual union and creation. Make a decision to stay in touch with your own sexuality as part of life's celebration. Sometimes we allow sex to become prescriptive and we neglect the poems, pictures, dances and stories.

## PACHAMAMA

Pachamama, or Mama Pacha, is from Peru in South America; she dates back to pre-Inca times, and is considered

the most revered goddess in the Andes. She is a goddess of earth and nature and agriculture, and she is regularly petitioned for a good harvest. Corn meal is sometimes poured onto the earth as an offering to her, accompanied by invocations from the women.

Pachamama can also be a dragon who may cause earthquakes by her movement just below the earth's shell. Llamas are sacrificed to her, possibly to propitiate her and prevent earthquakes. She is linked with her husband Inti, the sun god, Mama Cocha, the sea goddess, and the storm god, Illampu – an integration of all four elements.

## THE POWER OF THE EARTH

Pachamama is still revered in South American countries, where the fruits of the earth, food from different regions, are offered to her. She reminds us today of the need to acknowledge the power of the earth and of the occasional capricious nature of her elements.

# White Buffalo Calf Woman

White Buffalo Calf Woman is a wise woman and teacher to several tribes of Native Americans. Her inspirations and teachings still resonate with many Native Americans today. She is also known as White Buffalo Woman, White Buffalo Cow Woman, or White Buffalo Maiden.

White Buffalo Calf Woman brought the sacred medicine pipe, with the belief that tobacco united all the forces of nature in harmony and that spirits in the smoke of the pipe can grant wishes. She also brought several ceremonies, including the Sun Dance and the White Buffalo Ceremony.

The buffalo is a sign of affluence for the Native Americans; it teaches that everything is in abundance, but that

WHITE BUFFALO CALF WOMAN
CONNECT ME TO THE NATURAL WORLD
HELP ME TO PROTECT NATURE

the earth and nature must be respected. It is important to give thanks for all the gifts of nature, and to respect the animals that one hunts. Many indigenous groups practise what we now call 'environmentally friendly' lifestyles. They believe that establishing the right relationship between the elements of the natural and human world assures abundance.

A white buffalo is considered the most holy of creatures and the Lakota believe it indicates that a period of great wealth is about to begin. In 1994 a white buffalo calf was born to the Lakota tribe and it inspired great hope for changes in their lives.

When the buffalo were plentiful, they provided both food and leather for tipis; the sinews were used for sewing and the lard for cooking. Herds were decimated by poachers at the end of the nineteenth century and only in recent years are they being established once more.

If a hunter killed a rare white buffalo, he could only keep the animal if he had four sons, and he would then ask a virgin girl to clean the skin according to lengthy ritual practices. This meticulous procedure included alignment with the four winds and the four cardinal points of the earth. Eventually the skin would be laid out on ground from which every piece of grass had been removed, because only the bare earth can receive prayers. Finally it would be cut into strips and given to all the guests, who would keep them for life. They would never wear them for war but only for celebrations.

Native American mythology includes many stories that explore the relationship between people and buffaloes, each respecting the other's gifts and talents. Native American culture and shamanic rituals regulated attitudes and actions toward the natural world. We can learn from White Buffalo Calf Woman the care and detail that is necessary for our crafts. She reminds us to care for our environment, to take only what is reasonable, and to leave enough for those who may follow us.

# EARTH GODDESS *Stories* & EXERCISES

Earth goddesses bring us many images of growth, fertility, creativity and sexuality. They help us to establish security by putting down strong roots, which means we also have the freedom to explore new ideas and take risks. When we 'know where we are', we can then venture safely into unknown landscapes.

## WHITE BUFFALO CALF WOMAN'S STORY

*White Buffalo Calf Woman walked across the plains and entered the village, dressed in a white buckskin dress decorated with porcupine quills. She reminded the young warriors not to gaze upon her outer self but to acknowledge her inner spirit, like in the olden days. The tribe was surprised that she was such a young woman as they had expected a much older person. She entered the tepee, barefooted, and circled the fire seven times and then said that the fire burns forever in the heart of the Great Spirit, in the hearts of all living creatures, and the hearts of all human beings. She likened the tepee to the human body and its fire inside. However she warned against the destructive passion that roars out of control like a prairie fire. She then told them to fill the pipe with sacred tobacco and explained that the first breath would be gratitude for the Great Spirit, and the second breath is for your Mother, the earth: 'Give thanks for the grasses that clothe her breasts in prairies of flowing grain. Give thanks for the canopy of blue sky that she holds for you as a world in which to live. Give thanks for the storm clouds that bring rain to the prairies, filling creeks, water holes, springs and ponds.'*

(CAREY, 1991)

She explained that the subsequent breaths should be for all creatures, birds and fish, and for their own people that they should live in peace and not fight one another, and that they should then meditate upon six people whom they would like to see blessed. She then said that the seed she was planting would grow into the Tree of Understanding. Eventually it would be cut down in a dark storm from the east. Their Mother Earth would be bought, sold and stolen like a handful of beads. They must keep alight an ember, however small, which one day would be rekindled into a great fire. A new tree would grow, and would be even more glorious than the tree they had now:

*The Sacred Hoop will be mended, and the red, the yellow, the white and the black tribes, will live in harmony beneath the boughs of the new tree.*

Read through the story twice and think about six people that you would like to see blessed. They may be people close to you or estranged from you, people you have neglected or people you would like to join you on your path. Draw or paint your own tree of understanding, and place

your six people as fruits of your tree. Reflect on your picture and your six special people. Breathe in the images of the fruit of your tree, acknowledge each person as an individual, and give thanks for them. Choose one person of the six that you want to focus on and centre your healing thoughts on them. Concentrate on anything you think they may be in need of, and send it to them generously.

THE FOREST STORY
In a land far away, there is an aged forest with a river running through it, where the animals come to drink. The trees meet and form an arch over the river so that it looks like a shining green tunnel. The ancient trees tower above the vegetation, home to exotic birds. The undergrowth has layer upon layer, guarding the age-old secrets, healing the dark wounds from the past. The spirit of the beech tree is keeper of the forest. Blessed be.

After you have read the description of the ancient forest, create the forest in your imagination. Visualize every aspect of the vegetation, the trees and flowers, the river and the animals. Imagine you are one of the animals or birds of the forest. Write a story about life in this mysterious woodland.

**A PRAYER OF LIFE**
SILVER BIRCH STAY BEAUTIFUL
LADY OF THE WOODS IS WANTED
BLACKTHORN KEEP OUR DARKNESSES AT BAY
HAWTHORN LEAD US JOYOUSLY TO MAY
RED ROWAN KEEP OUR FIRES ALIGHT
FOR DANCING
GUARDIAN YEW ALLOW US EASE OF PASSING

# Air

Air is the least visible of the four elements and we experience it with senses other than sight. We can feel the light breezes or be blown around by storms. We can breathe in sweet, perfumed air or turn away from foul stenches. Air can be a powerful force: hurricanes or sea-storms can wreck houses and ships. But when there is no wind at all, we may feel oppressed by the lack of breeze. Air is a powerful force in our own bodies and is essential for life. Meditation and yoga are based on breathing routines to maximize our energy. Our breath is an indicator of our mood – it quickens when we are anxious or afraid and it slows when we are relaxed and when we sleep.

*Bring* with thee AIR from heaven or BLASTS from hell.

HAMLET, I.IV.41

# GODDESSES & *Air*

Goddesses are associated with air through the weather and the winds; sometimes the elements are said to be the moods of the goddess. Goddesses and witches may fly through the air, ride the storms or cause tempests to rage. Goddesses and female shamans may also use their breath to create new life and to heal.

### ILMATER

Ilmater, known as Daughter of the Air, is the Finnish goddess of creation, who created the universe. In the beginning there was only air and water, and Ilmater would float through the ether. Eventually she became very lonely. She landed on the waters, which became big waves from her winds, and she became pregnant. She created the sky and the earth and all the constellations from the eggs of primeval birds. She then gave birth to a son, who was the very first shaman.

### GODDESSES OF THE WIND

Native American peoples have many goddesses associated with the wind. Naayanxatisei, from the Plains, is known as Whirlwind Woman. She helped to create the world by spinning a piece of mud to make the land. Her name also means 'caterpillar' and caterpillars are believed to cause whirlwinds. She is also associated with physical strength because she threw a seductive deity into a stream.

Wind Woman, or Niarimamau, is a lustful goddess attracted to young men. She stole Dove's son and hid him in a cave and when he flew away she was trapped in the cave herself.

Many wind stories are also associated with birds; some of the

goddesses change into birds in some aspects. Ixlexwani is a sky goddess from the Northwest who flew to earth as a golden eagle with her sister and brothers. They brought with them beaver as a gift of food. Her siblings agreed to change into human people but she refused and wandered over the earth confused and distressed. Eventually her siblings killed her and she was turned into stone, petrified in a valley that has been named after her. Her petrification causes the coldest winter winds of all to blow. Her valley is known as the starting point for very bleak weather. Ixlexwani's story is about flexibility and reminds us that sometimes we need to change, before the cold wind of our lives keeps others at bay.

An Inuit story from the Arctic concerns three children who cause storms. Kadlu jumps on the ice to create huge rumbles of thunder, Kweeto makes the lightning by rubbing flints, and another child makes the rain by urinating. Many of the goddesses who are responsible for the weather occur in threes, like the Inuit children.

## AN IROQUOIS WIND GODDESS

Gusts-of-wind from the Iroquois was the daughter of the sky god, Chief-who-holds-the-earth, and the earth goddess, Araentsic. Gusts-of-wind married the wind-ruler and became pregnant with twins. Sadly she died before they were born because the twin boys were enemies and were already fighting in the womb. After Gusts-of-wind died, her mother created the sun and the moon out of her body and hid them beneath the earth's surface.

## LISTEN TO THE WIND

When you think about the wind, do you hide from the storm or do you walk in nature and feel uplifted? Although the recent hurricanes devastated so much countryside, many people felt empowered to review their lives. They felt that the storms could not be controlled and that they had to acknowledge the magnificence and supremacy of nature. Whether it is the calm breeze or the mighty tempest, let us pause to acknowledge a powerful element in our lives.

Ilmater, known as Daughter of the Air, is the Finnish goddess of creation.

# Freya

Freya is the most revered of the Nordic goddesses; she teaches magic to the other gods and is sometimes known as the leader of the Valkyries, 'choosers of the slain' who conduct the souls of heroes killed in battle to Valhalla. She is a goddess of magic, creation, love, beauty and sexuality.

Freya sometimes wears a magnificent cloak of falcon feathers as she flies down to the underworld to gain information for her role as a seer. She rides across the skies in a chariot pulled by tom cats. After battles she goes with her warrior maidens to select the most handsome of the fallen men to dine with her in her banqueting hall. She also receives the souls of unmarried women.

The Norse dwarfs made beautiful necklaces, which Freya was determined to own. The dwarfs said that the only means to own the necklaces would be if she slept one night with each of them. Although she found them distasteful, she slept her way to the necklaces! Golden ambers are sacred to Freya and are sometimes described as her tears. Her sacred animals include the cat, falcon, swallow, cuckoo and sow. Her bird images ensure her freedom.

Freya is sometimes seen as another aspect of Frigg, who is known as a beloved wife, or spouse, and as a mother, family and earth goddess. She was mistress of the home crafts and her symbols are the spindle and the distaff. Her sacred animals are the ram, spider and heron. Freya and Frigg were both married to Odin. Freya was a goddess of sexual pleasure and was said to sleep with everyone, all the gods, mortals and giants. Frigg was the guardian of marriages and made them fruitful.

Freya's day is Friday and there are places in England named after her – Freefolk, Froyle, and Frobury in Hampshire, Fryup and Friydaythorpe in Yorkshire. She is an extrovert goddess who lives life to the full.

Freya and Frigg represent the two extremes: sexual pleasure and motherhood, and sometimes we have difficulty reconciling them. Let them be!

## FREYA REFLECTION

Take time to think about whether you are living your own life to the full or whether it has become a routine without inspiration for you. Think about Freya's wonderful cape made of falcon feathers and her necklaces of amber. Decide on a piece of clothing or jewellery that speaks of freedom for yourself. Perhaps invite others to a freedom meal and share your emblems, with wine and laughter.

# Hine titama, Hyrokkin & the Harpies

## HINE TITAMA

Hine titama is a dawn maiden goddess of the Maori people of New Zealand. She is associated with heaven and hell, families and tribes, love and sexuality. She is the daughter of Tane Mahuta,

god of the forest and birds, and Hine ahuone, 'earth-formed maid', with eyes that make the sunset red, and hair like seaweed. Hine titama's father wanted her to marry a young man that he approved of, and he realized that he wanted to take her for himself and marry her. He did not tell her his plans but changed himself into a young man. Hine titama married her father without realizing what was happening, and bore his children. However, the wind and the waves started to whisper words of doubt and in the end Hine titama listened to them. She confronted her father and insisted on the truth. Divine incest is common in many goddess myths, but Hine titama said it was not how she wanted to live her life. She fled to the underworld and became an underworld deity. Here she took the name Hine nui te po and she now welcomes new souls to the world of the dead.

### THE BIRTH OF DEATH

An important story is told about Hine titama, which explains why human people must be born, and then die. The hero Maui boasted to his bird friend that he could crawl into the goddess through her vagina, and then move up to her heart, which he would eat. By eating the heart of the goddess of death, he bragged, he himself would conquer death.

Maui turned himself into a small lizard and was about to enter the goddess's vagina when his bird companion burst out laughing. He was highly amused at the sight of his friend, who was supposed to be a hero, turning into a lizard and moving through Hine titama, now Hine nui te po's pubic hair! Unfortunately for Maui, the sound of the laughter woke the goddess, who crushed the hero between her thighs and he died. And so it was that all people must die and

And so it was that all people must die and be welcomed to the otherworld by the goddess of death. We need have no fear.

be welcomed to the otherworld by
the goddess of death. Another version
of the story tells how Maui entered
the goddess but got trapped in her
womb and was unable to return.

## HINE TITAMA'S GIFT

We can take strength from Hine titama.
She stood up to her own father, even
though she had to abandon her children,
determined not to go down a path she
thought was wrong. Her strength is
echoed by Lilith (see page 62), who stood
up to her spouse and insisted on equality.

This an important theme for
women. We may need strength to
challenge other people's assumptions. If
others impose stereotypes onto us, or
if we feel pressurized to choose a
career because it is expected of us by
teachers, family or friends, we can
invoke Hine titama. We may not be
able to change things overnight. Don't
let us live with the phrase 'if only'.

The goddesses in this book can
help you to make decisions about your
life. See what they all have to offer,
and then look at what your heart is
saying to you.

## THE HARPIES

The Harpies were originally Greek
storm goddesses, numbering anything
up to eight. They transformed into
monsters with female heads and
vulture-like bodies, and vulture's feet,
and were known as snatchers of
corpses. They may have developed
from the birds-of-prey goddesses of
ancient times. At several ancient sites
the remains of large numbers of birds
of prey have been found. Just the
bones from the wings of large carrion

birds were in one place. At other
sites, such as those in the Orkney
Isles, there are skeletons of eagles
(there are no vultures in Scotland),
many buried in a single megalithic
tomb. Cave paintings and stone
sculptures of vultures are found in
various parts of the world.

## DEATH CULTS

It would seem that in some cults
carrion 'birds of the dead' were
sacrificed to the goddess of the dead,

*Let us keep our wisdom as elder woman, and our strength of vision. But may we still find adventure and a joy in the unexpected.*

with whom the Harpies are linked. The Harpies contaminated their victims' food, inflicted divine punishment and carried the souls of the dead. Therefore the vulture, as a carrion bird, is connected with the death cults.

Cardea, the Roman goddess, also seems to be linked with the Harpies. She was known as the goddess of door hinges, and was described by the poet Ovid as the 'hinge of the world on which the seasons turn'. She is believed to control the four cardinal winds, and also guards children against night spirits who kidnap them and suck their blood.

However, earlier versions of Cardea's story suggest just the opposite. Cardea herself is a predatory goddess, described as a witch who can turn into a blood-sucking night bird or beast, who destroys children. The hawthorn tree is sacred to her. The custom of banning hawthorn from inside the house in case children are destroyed is still observed by many rural villages in Europe.

## HYROKKIN

Hyrokkin is a Nordic goddess of winter storms. She is a large hag who rides through the air on a wolf with a bridle made of snakes. She was once summoned by the gods because of her great strength. Balder, the son of the goddess Frigg, died, and he was mourned so much on earth that it stopped his funeral boat from travelling to the underworld. Hyrokkin was asked to help launch the ship and she arrived on her wolf, grim-faced, and with one push, the boat was freed and once more was on its way to the underworld. Thor became extremely angry with Hyrokkin, which was very unreasonable. She had just carried out a task they had requested: she had freed the boat on its way to the underworld.

## REFLECTIONS

The goddesses in this section carry images of death and old age, themes that we often find very scary. We do not want to age, and as we get older it means that death is approaching. Yet consider the sheer strength of the aged Hyrokkin. None of the gods could move the boat, and yet with one shove from her it was on its way!

We need positive role models as we age. Crones are elder women of wisdom and experience. They are represented by old moon, the moon in its last quarter, and they have more freedom than ever before. They can say and do what they like, just like 'the woman who wears purple and a red hat that doesn't match' with her satin shoes and gloves. She gobbles up the samples in shops! What a wonderful example for us as we get older.

Let us think about having a new adventure and perhaps travel to somewhere new, somewhere we have never visited before. Perhaps we can meet Hyrokkin's wolves in the mountains of Transylvania or see her snakes in temples in the Far East. We may be able to make a journey by train to the Orkney Islands and see the astonishing megalithic tombs. Life is for living right now, today, and we can take some risks! Endings will come at the right time, we do not need to be afraid.

# Lilith

Lilith is also called Lil in Sumerian texts; she is a queen of heaven, whose name means 'air' or 'storm'. Lil also means 'dust-storm' or 'dust-cloud', which suggests a connection with ghosts. She is sometimes said to represent the darker side of the goddess Inanna and her dark sister, Ereshkigal.

She is first mentioned in a poem about Inanna, when the hero Gilgamesh has cut down Inanna's tree:

*Gilgamesh struck the serpent who could not be charmed.*
*The Anzu-bird flew with his young to the mountains;*
*And Lilith smashed her home and fled to the wild, uninhabited places.*
(WOLKSTEIN AND KRAMER, 1983)

A stone relief from 2000 BCE shows a winged goddess with bird feet standing on a lion, flanked by two owls. She wears a horned crown and carries measuring rods. The lion, owls and goddess look straight ahead, and the lions lie on the sacred mountain. Some sources attribute this image to Lil, others to Inanna or Ishtar. But Lilith is known to be associated with kites and wolves, as well as with owls, who are harbingers of death.

In the Hebrew texts, Lilith is most popularly known as the first wife of Adam, who left him when he instructed her to lie beneath him when they made love. Lilith refused, pointing out that they had been created equal. Lilith went to Jehovah and tricked him into saying his secret name; with this power she was able to persuade him to give her wings, and she flew away to live in a cave by the sea. Lilith became the essence of depraved sexuality in Judaic mythology, described as being created from 'filth and impure sediment instead of dust or earth'. She was believed to steal semen when men were sleeping, which she used to fertilize herself, producing demons. Lilith was also believed to kill children, and mothers give their children amulets to protect them from her. A complete demonization of Lilith took place as she was incorporated into the Judaic pantheon.

## AN IMAGE OF HOPE

Lilith can offer us a vision of freedom and independence. We may wish to flee to wild and uninhabited places when the oppression surrounding us is too great. We all know women who have been demonized because they are independent beings, who refuse to be subordinate. Let us remember the oppression of women, past and present, and lend our support. Let us remind our friends about such women and light a candle in their honour.

# AIR GODDESS *Stories* & EXERCISES

Air has come to us in many forms through the stories of the goddesses and through our own reflections on our breathing and our bodies. Our breathing is literally our inspiration: as we breathe in, we inspire, we are living. We can also let the storms and the night riders jolt us into new ideas and pathways.

### ILMATER'S STORY

Ilmater is the daughter of the air and the ether. She came down to embrace the sea, and she stayed cradled and tossed by the waves for seven hundred years. The celestial duck laid seven eggs and Ilmater used them to create the rest of the universe. There was only water and air so she made the earth and the sky, the sun and the moon, and then the stars in the sky. When the universe was ready, she became pregnant from the wind and gave birth to three sons, one of whom was the first shaman. He went on to complete the creation of the world that Ilmater had started.

When you read this story through, think about the wonderful imagery of Ilmater cradled in the sea, and allow this and other images to inspire you to create a picture. Eggs appear in many stories and rituals about fertility, especially in creation stories, and also in spring rituals that are still practised. At Easter, Greeks eat hard-boiled eggs painted red and sometimes bake them in sweetened bread; the English roll painted eggs down hills and then eat them; in Romania people give each other exquisite hand-painted wooden eggs. Create your own beautiful egg through painting or using felt-tip pens. Draw a picture of an egg or model one in clay; you could decorate a hard-boiled egg or even embellish plain wooden eggs from a carpenter. This is your own beautiful creation inspired by Ilmater.

### CREATE YOUR OWN BIRD PICTURE

Sit quietly with your eyes closed and recall all the stories about air and the different sorts of birds. Allow yourself to float like the birds as you think about which bird you feel linked with: maybe a broad-winged bird of prey, maybe a smaller bird created by a shaman; maybe a bird from your own

garden, or from stories you read in childhood. Choose one bird to explore right now: picture it and everything connected with it. Open your eyes and decide how you are going to create it. Choose your materials with care. You may want to paint your bird, and find special paints. Maybe you would like to make a collage, either in the garden, on a tray with silver sand, or on card with glue. Collect beads, coloured glass, feathers, seashells, little stones, nutshells and anything else that appeals to you. Collect them with love and care. Create the outline of your bird and all the details, before you make anything permanent. Then decide if it will be kept outside or in the house. You may decide to plant your bird and see it grow. Create the shape with pebbles and then plant it with small bedding plants and herbs. It may take several days or weeks to finish your bird, but there is no hurry. Take joy in the creation. When you have finished, write about the creative journey. If you have made a temporary bird, take a photograph of it.

## MEDITATION

Give yourself time to think about creative journeys in your life. Do you want to flee away like Lilith to a remote place, or do you want to be cradled on the sea like Ilmater? Think about phrases like 'whistle up the wind', 'blow away the cobwebs', 'riding the storm', 'it's an ill wind', 'blowing in the wind'.

Allow the wind goddesses to give you energy, allow them to inspire you, allow them to let you fly to new landscapes. Sit quietly and listen to the breezes or the storms, listen to your own breathing, and breathe in your new experiences.

# SECTION 2

## AN INTRODUCTION TO THE HEAVENLY BODIES

The stars, moon and sun are essential for our world to exist. How much time do we give to their contemplation, to allow them to give us an orientation in our lives? Many of us spend much energy sun-chasing and despair of short summers. Seasonal depression causes very real suffering, and many people need more light in their lives, in reality or symbolically. Star-gazing on a clear night is a very soothing pastime, and many stories are associated with stars and their names. Ariadne's constellation is the result of a troubled story, when she was abandoned by Theseus after helping him overcome the Minotaur.

The moon regulates our time and tides; our calendar is based on the moon's phases and regulates our menstrual cycle. We can find stability in the moon's repeating phases and think about her many faces. Always remember to give the old moon enough attention and then she treats us wisely, otherwise she can be a rabid bitch! Above all, the moon illuminates our path with a gentle light.

The sun is necessary for warmth and light, for crops to grow and for ourselves to play. The shedding of winter clothes – 'ne'er cast a clout 'til May be out' – gives our limbs a freedom we had forgotten during winter's darkness. We may have a favourite constellation, which leads us to a goddess who is important to us, but the heavenly bodies are all needed in different ways.

*Flow, flow, you HEAVENLY blessings, on her!*

*CYMBELINE, 3.v.167*

# Stars

There was a STAR danced,
and under THAT was I born.

*MUCH ADO ABOUT NOTHING, 2.1.340*

Throughout the ages we have thought about stars in so many ways: in the heavens, in the media, as a guide. Astrology is one of the oldest means of divination and prediction: stars seem to make life more secure in this uncertain world. We can experience our own place in the universe by looking up at the night sky. Sometimes the sky seems to have tiny holes with the stars shining through; when the sky is very clear, we see the vast expanse of a star-studded canopy, apparently continuing forever. Many of our goddesses have become stars and constellations, and in this form they continue to guide us.

# GODDESSES & *Stars*

Stars are a part of the lives of many goddesses, especially those with the title of Queen of Heaven, like Inanna and Aphrodite, and those that became stars, like Ariadne. The star goddesses are believed to be eternal. They are always in the heavens: unlike the sun and the moon they are constant and unchanging.

The Ona people of South America tell the following story of their creation by Star Creator. Long before there were people on the earth, it was inhabited by enormous giants with white beards. The Sun and Moon were husband and wife and lived on the earth with the giants. The giants began to fight each other, and the situation worsened, so the Sun and Moon left the earth for the skies. The Star Creator sent down the Red Star who killed all the giants. Then Star Creator took two lumps of clay and created a man and a woman: the ancestors of the Ona people.

The Red Star is thought to be the planet Mars, who of course displays warlike qualities in many stories; this quality is captured in the music of the *The Planets*, by Gustav Holst.

EVENINGSTAR

Eveningstar of Wakaranga is a Rhodesian goddess who gave birth to domestic animals, children and also antelopes and birds. Later she created wild animals including lions, tigers and reptiles. She shares her responsibilities with Morningstar. According to myth, Eveningstar is chased by Moon across the sky every night because he is angry that she sent a snake to bite him. Moon becomes ill and the land is plagued by famine and drought, and the crops fail. The people decide it is Moon's fault that there is no food or water and the cattle are dying. They capture him, strangle him and then throw him into the ocean. Moon continues to rise from the ocean and chase Eveningstar across the sky.

TARA

The goddess Tara appears in many manifestations in the religions and philosophies of Asia. Buddhist, Hindu, Jain, Tibetan and Tantric beliefs all accord her a high status.

'Around her shines a halo of spirit in which the animal principle of the lower world, beginning with the lion, is transformed into a vegetal light, into the grown and growing illumination characteristic of her being. In her hands she holds flowers and above her is spread the fiery canopy of light strewn with silver star blossoms.'
(NEUMANN, 1963)

A compassionate deity, she was born from a tear of Avalokita, one who reached the highest understanding.

Tara is the guide through the stages of life, and is sometimes seen as the boat woman who leads us across from the 'churning sea' of this world, to the sublime 'nirvana' of the heavens. White Tara is pictured as sublime womanhood, enthroned on her lotus seat.

Tara is a compassionate goddess who can also be playful. As Green Tara she can be quite frightening, but she can be invoked to help with seemingly impossible difficulties, before we decide to give up! Because she is a goddess of self-mastery she can inspire us to continue, even though the going is tough.

## STARGAZING

Pause in your busy life and stargaze. Find the seven stars of Ariadne, the Milky Way and the Pleiades. See if you can read the stars in the heavens and let them illuminate your path. Make a wish if you see a shooting star!

# Inanna

Inanna has many names, including Queen of Heaven, Morning and Evening Star, Moon Goddess, Goddess of the Grain and the Green One. She is an ancient goddess of Sumeria and her stories, which were discovered written on seals, are probably the oldest myths to have been written down.

Many themes from her tales, such as her descent into the underworld, and the death and regeneration of the flora, are echoed in later myths and stories in ancient Greece and in the Old and New Testaments. As Queen of Heaven and Morning and Evening Star, Inanna rules the heavens, especially at daybreak and twilight. She is 'clothed with the heavens and crowned with the stars'; she wears the rainbow as her necklace and the zodiac as her belt. Her gemstone is lapis lazuli, which is blue like the sky.

Inanna had to make a journey into the underworld to meet her dark sister, Ereshkigal, who killed her and hung her on a meat peg. Inanna was rescued through her friend Ninshubar and the interventions of the trickster, Enki. He modelled two little figures from clay and spittle, who slipped into the underworld with food and water for Ereshkigal. While Inanna was away, the land was barren; fertility was restored when she returned to earth. Many poems are attributed to Inanna, including those to her lover Dumuzi.

I OVERCOME THE FLOOD
I RIDE THE STORM DRAGON
INTO THE RAGING WINDS

I KNOW THE ART OF WOMEN
AND CREATE EXQUISITE
POETRY FOR MY LOVE

MY WOMB IS FERTILE AND
ABUNDANT, BRINGING FORTH
PLENTEOUS FRUIT AND LEGUMES

I KNOW THE DARK JOURNEY
THE NETHERWORLD HOLDS
NO FEAR FOR ME

## A MEDITATION ON INANNA

Sit in a comfortable place and close your eyes. Visualize yourself waking up in the morning, perhaps typically on a day when you would rather stay in bed. Imagine opening the curtains and seeing the sky as it appears just before dawn. Breathe in as you gaze out of your window and look for the morning star of Inanna, shining like a beacon. Allow her star to give you light for the coming day. Open your eyes and see if your energy has changed. Plan to repeat the exercise in real life the next day.

# Ariadne, Nut & Evening Star Woman

### ARIADNE

Ariadne was the daughter of Minos, the King of Crete. Minos in earlier years needed to settle a dispute with his brother. He prayed to the sea god, Poseidon, to send him a bull as a sign that the throne rightly belonged to him; he promised he would then sacrifice the bull. Poseidon sent a magnificent white bull, and Minos liked it so much that he sacrificed another bull instead. Poseidon was so angry he caused the Queen to have passionate feelings for the bull. The bull mated with her and she became pregnant. She gave birth to a boy with the head and tail of a bull and the body of a man, the Minotaur. He was concealed in a labyrinth, deep in the ground. Every eight years, the King of Athens sent to Minos seven girls and seven boys, who were sacrificed to the Minotaur. One year Theseus, son of the King of Athens, was among the seven. On arrival in Crete he met Ariadne, and she agreed to help him kill the Minotaur. She gave him a sword and a ball of thread, and he tied the thread to the door lintel. He unravelled the thread as he went deep into the labyrinth, killed the Minotaur and found his way back again with the thread. Ariadne and Theseus sailed away, making for Athens. They stopped on the island of Naxos and while Ariadne was asleep, Theseus abandoned her and sailed on.

There are various endings to this story. One is that Ariadne was rescued by Poseidon and turned into a cluster of stars; she can now be seen in the sky as the seven stars of Ariadne. Another reports that Dionysus saw her, fell in love with her, and they married and had three sons.

We can think about this story as an enactment of an older story of a ritual marriage between the priestess-queen and priest-king, wearing the cow and bull horned masks. Ariadne was originally a Minoan goddess, but later Greeks considered her mortal, with diminished power.

You could write your own ending to the story, explaining how Ariadne felt after being abandoned by the man she loved, and how she took strength and changed her future.

### NUT

Nut is an Egyptian goddess of the celestial firmament. Also known as Mystery of the Heavens and The Starry One, she is often represented as the heavenly cow. She is the mother of Horus, Osiris, Set, Isis and Nephthys. Ra decided to abandon earth and asked Nut to take him up into the heavens. Carrying him on her back, she rose higher and higher, and she became very dizzy. She would have crashed to the ground if four gods had

Ariadne was originally a Minoan goddess.

*Star Woman give me the strength to challenge ridicule and walk away from broken promises. Let me not be bullied away from my chosen star path.*

not supported her, and Shu held up her belly. The four gods became the pillars of the sky, and Ra hung the stars on Nut's body, which is shaped in a permanent arch. Stars can live for only twelve hours, so Nut continually renews them all and gathers them in her pear-shaped vessel.

### EVENING STAR WOMAN

Evening Star Woman is the most beautiful goddess of all to the Northeast Native Americans. She rules the stars and the planets, and the calendar men make notches in their sticks when she rises.

The story goes that she ran away with Thunderbird. Everyone was very angry that she had gone, so the Great Spirit caught the Thunderbird. He found Evening Star Woman and placed her back in the sky in her rightful place.

### THE STORY OF STAR WOMAN

The Bush People of South Africa believe that there is a race of people who live in the stars. They are a happy and contented people, who want for nothing except for milk. Every so often the Star Women come down to earth, with their unique baskets on their backs, and a bucket in their hand, to take the milk from a farmer's cows. Every Star Woman has her own individual back-basket, which is given to her at birth; it is a beautiful shape, gorgeously coloured and has a tight-fitting lid; in it each Star Woman keeps her most treasured secrets.

One day a farmer who lived all alone noticed that his milk was disappearing. He would go out in the morning to milk the cows and there would be very little there. When he had discovered this several times, he was determined to find out what was happening. When it got dark, he hid in some bushes at the edge of the field and gazed for hours into the dark. He was getting cold and stiff, and was about to give up, when he heard some sounds far away. It was the sound of women chatting and giggling together, as they got nearer and nearer to the earth. He peered round the bush and saw the group of women with their basket and buckets, and he ran toward them, longing to speak.

When the Star Women saw him, they turned and ran back to their silver threads and started being pulled toward the sky – except for one woman, who tripped and fell, and her silver thread disappeared. The farmer went up to her and asked her to stay with him on his farm, and she agreed on one condition. As long as he

promised never to look in her basket, she would come and live with him. She settled down reasonably well; she tended her garden and helped on the farm. Sometimes in the evening she would stand in the doorway and gaze up at the stars, wondering how her family was, and whether she was missed. She felt a little homesick.

After the first few days, the farmer began to get curious about the basket which was standing in the corner of their sitting room. Soon he could contain himself no longer, and when he thought Star Woman was out of the

way, he went to look in the basket. Star Woman appeared in the doorway: 'But you promised!' she said. The farmer turned, and laughed: 'But there is nothing there!' he said. Star Woman turned on her heel and left the house. She reached the gate and looked back one more time. The silver thread was waiting for her, and she went back up to her people in the sky. The issue was not that the farmer had looked in the basket, even though he had promised not to. It was that he could not even see what the basket contained and had laughed as if the basket did not matter,

### STAR WOMAN'S BASKET

When you have read through the story of Star Woman a couple of times, think about her decision to return to the stars because of the farmer's foolishness. Would you have done the same? Think about her basket, and imagine what would be inside the one that you might have, what most treasured things would you keep in it? Draw a picture of a unique back-basket, with a tightly fitting lid and back-straps. Create its special colours and shapes. Who might have given it to you, and why? Allow this picture to be a gift to yourself.

# Venus

Venus is a gentle goddess of sensual love. She protects gardens and vineyards and likes order in her landscape. She was beloved of the Romans, who adorned her with roses. Venus is the goddess of herbs, strawberries and cypress trees. Her colour is green and her jewel is the emerald.

Venus' name comes from the Latin words for loving veneration. She is thought to have been the partner of Mars, the god of war, and mother of Aeneas, the founder of Rome. There is a large temple to her in Rome, situated on the Circus Maximus, and she is celebrated at her festival of Vinalia Priora on 23 April.

Venus was known to the Greeks as Aphrodite, the goddess of love and sexuality. One of the twelve Olympian divinities, she was revered both on the Greek mainland and in Cyprus, although she is of Phoenician origin. Aphrodite's name means 'foam', which may link her with Botticelli's painting, *The Birth of Venus*. Aphrodite is believed to have the gift of prophecy and to be a champion in war.

Venus has inspired painters, musicians, playwrights and poets, and is the only female star to be included in Holst's musical constellations. Many of her images have changed from those of love to those of sexuality, as can be seen in paintings from the seventeenth century onward, such as *The Triumph of Venus*. This shows her naked, appearing to a group of men from different periods of history, all of whom had the reputation of being great lovers.

Many ancient figurines have been given the name of Venus, such as the Venus of Willendorf and the Venus of Laussel, even though they have no relationship with the Roman goddess at all. The name Venus seems now to be used generally as a female title, rather than as the name of a specific individual goddess.

Venus, like the other star goddess Inanna, is associated with the morning star and the evening star, which shines particularly brightly at the transitions between the day and the night. Venus shines brighter as the sky grows pale.

## A HERB GARDEN DEDICATED TO VENUS

Venus is the goddess of herbs who also likes order in her landscape. Create a traditional herb spiral in your garden, with a bay tree at the centre. Or plant large pots with several herbs in a circle. Crush a leaf in your hand each day and take time to inhale its heady perfume. Pick fresh herbs for your cooking, salads and tea. Use your herbs with reverence.

# STAR GODDESS *Stories* & EXERCISES

Star goddesses illuminate many aspects of our lives, an echo of our ancient past. Maybe we forget our celestial heritage when we popularize 'stars': stars in our eyes, stars in the media, saying to someone 'you are a star!'. Next time we award a star to someone, maybe one of our children, remember its archaic past and give it real meaning, give it star quality.

## INANNA'S STORY

The journey of the ancient Sumerian goddess Inanna takes her into the darkness and then into light, a journey of suffering and then rejoicing.

Inanna, Queen of the Heavens, went to the underworld to meet her dead sister Ereshkigal, Queen of the Great Below. Before she left she asked her helper, Ninshubar, to summon help from the gods if she did not return in three days When. Inanna arrived at the gates of the underworld, the keeper announced her to her sister. Ereshkigal was very angry and ordered Inanna to arrive naked and bowed low. She had to remove one piece of jewellery or clothing at each gate and crawl into the presence of her sister. Freshkigal killed her and left her corpse hanging on a peg to turn green.

Ninshubar was worried that Inanna had not returned and went in search of help, shouting, singing and beating a drum. The earth had turned barren, and the land was parched. The gods

would not listen, as they did not want to interfere with the rules of the underworld. In desperation Ninshubar turned to Enki, god of water and wisdom. He created two little figures from the dirt under his fingernails, and sent them into the underworld with water and bread to console Ereshkigal. She released Inanna alive, and Inanna returned to the Great World Above, reclaiming her fine apparel on the way. She had to send a substitute as a sacrifice to the underworld. Meanwhile it was a time of great celebration as the earth again became fertile and Inanna returned to her rightful place as Queen of Heaven.

*Weave my tales into song,*
*Flowing from ear to mouth,*
*Flowing from old to young,*
*Inanna, Queen of Heaven.*

## INANNA ACTIVITIES

As you read Inanna's story, think about this journey of a woman going into the darkness, made very vulnerable by the removal of all the trappings that gave her both her office

and her identity. Think about your journey in life and ask yourself whether you carry any things that get in the way of you moving forward.

Share this exercise with a friend and discuss the symbolic clothes we may have inherited from our past, for example our mother's tight dress that does not allow us to breathe, or our father's hat that restricts our vision. This is an exercise for reflecting on personal freedom, to help let go of the ties that inhibit, and so wear our creative sashes with joy.

Create a dance of freedom with a group of friends, to celebrate your return to the fertile land. You can create poems and chants inspired by Inanna, and maintain this feeling of freedom and lightness as you break free from your chains!

### FRIENDSHIP

The image of Enki, who assisted in Inanna's rescue when the other gods and goddesses refused to do so, is very touching. Think about the two little figures that he created out of dirt – ultimately it is the little

creatures who can slip in unawares that help Inanna, not the powerful deities or the noisy drum. Charity shops sell tiny little Guatemalan 'worry dolls': people tell them their concerns and then put them under their pillows. Acquire something similar for yourself, or make them out of clay and place them where you can see them every day. Remind yourself that small is beautiful and notice small things – children see ants and find them wondrous.

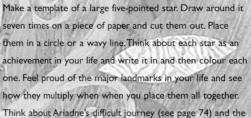

### ARIADNE'S STARS

Make a template of a large five-pointed star. Draw around it seven times on a piece of paper and cut them out. Place them in a circle or a wavy line. Think about each star as an achievement in your life and write it in and then colour each one. Feel proud of the major landmarks in your life and see how they multiply when when you place them all together. Think about Ariadne's difficult journey (see page 74) and the ending you wrote for her story. Does it have links with your own story? Reflect on how Ariadne's story connects with the picture of your stars.

TAKE TIME FOR THE STARS, TAKE TIME FOR THE SMALL THINGS.
FIND PEACE IN STAR GAZING, FIND PEACE IN SMALL THINGS.

# Moon

The Moon is one of the most important symbols for women — it traces our cycle of life through new moon, full moon, old moon, or maiden, mother, crone. It completes its journey every month, like our menstrual pattern. The moon influences the tides and the full moon gives us a gentle glowing light, which illuminates our path without blinding our eyes. The wolf, with its stable family and social grouping, is linked with the moon, and the wolf and the moon are common totems. Let us hold on to our positive moon images — the gentle strength in her silver-grey light, the moonbeams that light us on our way, and the waters of the moon that lull us into a sweet dream life.

The MOON shines bright in such a night as this, When the sweet WIND did gently kiss the trees.

*MERCHANT OF VENICE, 5.1.1*

# GODDESSES & THE *Moon*

Moon goddesses are usually goddesses of fertility as well as of procreation and the female life cycle. Many of them are also goddesses of the heavens, stars, sea or floods. Moon, the night sky and the oceans are thus integrated into a single goddess. Many stories connect the sun and the moon as partners or enemies.

In the story The Buried Moon (see page 94), the moon is a kindly presence in the heavens, with so much concern for the human race and their vicissitudes that she comes down to earth, with terrifying consequences.

Dahomean Moon Woman is a moon goddess from the Benin people of Gambia; she is also Moon and Night, Mother and Guardian. The Benin tell a story about Sun and Moon and their children the Stars. Sun would go out in the day with his star children, and Moon was very anxious because she thought it was far too hot

for them. She decided to protect them by making sure that they only came out at night. Sun was very angry at what Moon had done and he spends his time chasing Moon across the sky. Sometimes he catches her, which is when there is an eclipse.

Another Gambian group, the Serer, also have a Dahomean Moon Woman myth. In their story, Sun and Moon are out together and happen to pass by a waterfall where their mothers are bathing. Sun looks away but Moon stares at the women bathing. God decided to make Sun bright so that

people would know about his modest behaviour. He deliberately made Moon dimmer than the sun so that people would stare at her, just as she had stared at her mother.

These moon goddess stories from Gambia seem very practical stories about day-to-day life, creating social rules of how people ought to behave. Children should not be in the heat, it is not good for them. You must not stare at your mother's nudity. This social level of the stories is very different from the symbolic, mythic qualities of some of the other goddess tales, and makes a refreshing change. The following story from Polynesia is very different indeed.

Hina is a creator deity and moon goddess from Polynesia. She lives in the moon and is the patron of tapa, a patterned native cloth that has spiritually protective qualities. She is the wife and daughter of Tii, and together they created the first humans.

*Hina set out to find the prince of her dreams and she asked the sea creatures to help her. They failed and Hina*

became extremely angry. She beat the flounder flat and put both its eyes on the same side; the rock cod's head was beaten to a pulp; she then made a lump on the turtle's back, and split the whale's tail by throwing a coconut at it. She then walked away and sailed to the moon in a canoe. She stepped into the moon and never returned to the earth again.

(BASED ON ANN AND IMEL, 1993)

REFLECTIONS

These moon stories are very varied and include partnerships as well as strife. The moon can be concerned and gentle or she can have a terrifying, violent aspect. The story of Hina tells of anger and gratuitous violence against the sea creatures when she is thwarted from finding her handsome prince. The story is not a blueprint for violence, rather it is a means of us being able to think about our own anger. Perhaps we can allow the characters in the stories to be angry on our behalf. One way of looking at stories and plays is that they express things that we are unable to, either because it is too frightening to do so, or because it is not socially acceptable.

# Artemis/Diana

Artemis, the moon goddess, the Lady of Beasts and the virgin huntress, is known as the protector of childbirth and wild animals. She had an extensive following in Greece, but earlier she was the warrior goddess of the Amazons. She can also appear as a bear, the moon, a nymph and a tree.

Artemis is described by many poets and playwrights. The following is from Aeschylus' play *Agamemnon*:

*Artemis, lovely Artemis, so kind*
*to the ravening lion's tender, helpless cubs,*
*the suckling young of beasts that stalk*
   *the wilds.*
*bring this sign for all its fortune,*
*all its brutal torments home to birth.*

Many small shrines at springs are dedicated to Artemis all over the Greek landscape, and some villages still honour her 'little bear cult', when small girls would become the little bears of Artemis and attend on her at the shrines. Adult maidens also accompanied her on her hunts, and in her Temple at Ephesus she would have 'bee-maidens' called the Melisai.

As with many of the goddesses, Artemis has an equivalent in Roman mythology, although their attributes are not identical. Diana is a Roman and Sabine goddess, whose name means 'growth'. She is also a goddess of the moon, women, procreation and birth, and hunting. Her chief festival is the Festival of Candles, celebrated on 15 August, when her sacred groves would be ablaze. Candles are still lit on this date but now it is to celebrate the Christian feast of the Assumption of Mary.

Although Artemis protects wild animals, she also hunts them and takes pleasure in the hunt. Hunters would drape the horns and the skin of an animal on a tree in thanksgiving to Artemis. However, she would punish anyone who carelessly slew pregnant or suckling animals.

Artemis and Diana are champions of women to this day, and are evoked for strength and independence from a male-dominated world. Some women took Princess Diana to their hearts as a symbol of the goddess who had been wronged and sacrificed. Artemis and Diana are both invoked at childbirth, to help ease the labour as a new and blessed life is born.

Homer's *Hymn to Artemis* describes her as having a golden bow and arrows that moan; the poem opens with the following:

ARTEMIS I SING
WITH HER GOLDEN ARROWS
AND HER HUNTING CRY
THE SACRED MAIDEN
DEER-HUNTRESS
SHOWERING ARROWS

# Arianrhod, Bendis & Anahita

## ARIANRHOD

Arianrhod is a Welsh goddess of the moon, fate and fertility, whose name means 'Silver Wheel'. This refers to the circumpolar stars, Caer Arianrhod, which never set below the horizon' (elaborated in Farrar and Bone, 2000),

the resting-place for souls before reincarnation. Her silver wheel is the turning wheel of fate. It can also be the divine spinning wheel, weaving the web of destiny. Much of her early history is obscure but we know that her castle, also called Caer Arianrhod, is supposed

to lie submerged in Caernarvon Bay, and is still marked on maps.

Although she said she was a virgin goddess, she went on to have two children, Lleu and Dylan. It is interesting that with many goddesses the issue of virginity is not to do with sexual behaviour but with 'belonging to a man'; but in this story it is an issue that has to be 'proved'. Arianrhod tried to prevent Lleu from gaining his birthright, which was a name, arms and a wife; Lleu outwitted her with the help of her poet brother, Gwydian, who was also Lleu's father. Arianrhod was later relegated to the role of sorceress. Opinion is divided as to whether this comes about with the rise of male-led beliefs rather then female. However, her celestial silver wheel in the submerged castle in Wales is still remembered to this day.

## BENDIS

The great moon goddess Bendis is honoured in Thrace, Greece, Dacia and now Romania. The Thracians revered the forces of nature, worshipped the sun and believed in the immortality of the soul. Their mythology included Bendis, the sacred Horsemen, Dionysus and Orpheus. Bendis is depicted holding a twig, which links her with vegetation, and she is a hunting goddess. She also has an aspect connected with the underworld. Her name means 'to bind', which links her with the stability of marriage. She is represented as a full-figured woman with prominent cheek bones and curly hair, either plaited into two long plaits or made into large curls around her face.

Bendis is pictured between two sacred animals, either two deer or a buck and a snake. She is sometimes depicted riding a doe, bow in hand and with a quiver of arrows on her back. She hunts in the wild mountainous landscape, where the horse is sacred and the mysterious Thracian horsemen dispense life and

*Bendis lead me through the forests. Bendis lead me to the mysteries. Let me ride the sacred horse.*

*The spinning wheel of my life gives me shapes and patterns. Let me stay with its rhythm, stay with its creation. Let me stay with its creation and colour.*

death. She was adored by Thracian women for embodying the goddess of the moon, forests and magical charms. Bendis was adopted into Athenian festivities, festivals and races and amorous rites. It is here we find the links with Dionysus, and there is a suggestion of an orgiastic aspect to the worship of Bendis, as in the Dionysus revels.

## ANAHITA

Anahita is a Persian moon and fertility goddess, the most popular of seven major deities. Her following originated in Babylonia and her traditions spread to Egypt. She is adorned in gold: she wears a golden scarf, gold earrings and a jewelled crown. Her cloak is made from thirty-two otter skins that are embroidered with gold.

She is described by the Zoroastrians as being 'extraordinarily tall and strong, with a commanding appearance and heavily jewelled "according to the rule". Anahita was the divine energy for good which was thought to flow through the kings of Iran' (Husain, 1997). She protected them from their northern invaders. Anahita also has a war aspect. She is a virgin warrior goddess, who rides in a chariot across the skies, pulled by four white horses: wind, rain, cloud and hail. Anahita has celestial fountains in her stars; they pour water into the earth to make it fertile. She is also the guardian of human conception, fertility and childbirth, and she purifies both the womb and sperm. She is linked with sacred sexuality and divine union.

## SELENE

Selene, the full-moon goddess, drives a lunar chariot pulled by two white horses. She is known as Mistress of the Stars. She is associated with the first day of the waning moon. She falls in love with a human lover, Endymion, who has won the prize of eternal youth with Selene's help. She puts him into a deep sleep in his cave, and goes to see him frequently. They are reputed to have fifty daughters. Selene is the queen of high tides of rivers and seas.

### MOON GODDESS INSPIRATIONS

Arianrhod gives us the idea of the spinning wheel or weaving the tapestry of our lives. We can create a silver wheel to hang in our room to catch the candlelight. Think about your silver wheel: let it inspire you to 'spin a story' about your favourite goddess. Let Anahita give you a golden gift of some beads or cloth or a scarf. Enjoy the shining qualities: wear your scarf or beads, or wrap yourself in your cloth. Feel confident in your special clothes.

MOON HERBS AND HEALING

Many of the moon goddesses are linked with healing, especially healing through herbs. Many of the herbs are traditionally picked by moonlight in order to be at their most effective. You can grow herbs in your garden or buy pure herbs at health-food shops. Try to use fresh dried herbs: their healing is more potent.

Vervain is one of the herbs associated with moon healing. Steep dried vervain in hot water and drink this soothing tea with a little honey. It helps insomnia and can lull you to sleep. It also has a calming influence on relationships. It is used for purification and protection.

You can make a healing gift for someone who is unwell. Make a green or blue pouch of dried tansy for the person to wear or place under their pillow. It can be mixed with rosemary or eucalyptus for intensive healing.

Yarrow and Lavender can be dried and placed around your house for healing and protection. They are sweet-smelling and will lightly perfume a room. You may also try burning lavender essential oil in your oil burner while relaxing in your bath. Lavender is one of the most calming oils.

ESSENCE OF THE MOON

Think of all the different qualities of the moon goddesses and decide which one is speaking to you. Find out all you can about your favourite moon goddess and reflect on why she is helpful to you. Will she be a long-term companion or is she special at this time to assist with a current difficulty? There are goddess groups who meet at festivals and celebrations, in particular at equinox and solstice. Many of these groups revere a particular goddess. Or you could start your own group with your friends. Let it be a group for support and communication and for creative ways to explore goddess wisdom.

# Rhiannon

Rhiannon is a Welsh Celtic goddess of the moon who rides on a beautiful white mare. Flocks of birds surround her, welcoming in the seasons. She has several associations, including links with the sun and the otherworld. She was probably a goddess of fertility, Rigantona, from an earlier period.

Rhiannon is pursued by Prince Pwyll on horseback, and however fast he rides he cannot catch up with her! Yet she does not seem to be going fast at all, reminding us of the moon, which we can never capture. However, Rhiannon does marry Pwyll and they have a son, born on May Day. During the night the baby is kidnapped, and Rhiannon's attendants are scared they will be blamed. They kill a puppy and smear Rhiannon with blood to make it seem as if she has killed her own child. As a punishment she has to greet any person coming to the palace, tell them of her wicked deed and then carry them on her back into the great hall. Symbolically she is made to be a horse, carrying a burden. This punishment continues for some years.

Rhiannon's baby had been stolen by a demon, who then went to steal a horse. The farmer pursued the demon, who dropped the baby. Since he and his wife were childless they decided to keep the baby as if it were their own. However, they heard the

RHIANNON, GIVE ME
THE WISDOM TO LET
GO OF THE PAST,
STRENGTHEN THE
PRESENT AND
ILLUMINATE THE FUTURE

story of Rhiannon losing her baby and brought the child back to the palace. Rhiannon rejoiced in tears when her child was restored to her, showing that she had not committed such a terrible deed after all.

In later times Rhiannon was called an enchantress, and her magical birds can waken the dead and make the living have a sleep of seven years.

We also know Rhiannon as a sovereignty goddess, and kings were made by sacred marriage at Arberth.

### REFLECTIONS

Take courage from Rhiannon, who was wrongly accused and suffered several burdened years. I am sure we all know people, including ourselves, who have been wrongly accused by people in authority, or by gossipy neighbours. Children and vulnerable people are especially prone to these painful incidents. Let us care for them.

# MOON GODDESS *Stories* & EXERCISES

Moon goddesses lead us into the darker areas with a gentle torch. They allow us to have shadows until we are ready to explore them. They protect us in times of conflict with their shield, and hold our hopes and fears at childbirth. We need to revere moon goddesses in their many aspects as they speak to different stages in our lives.

### THE BURIED MOON

In times long ago, the land was boggy and unsafe and a treacherous place to walk. During the three dark nights of the moon, the bog became even more treacherous, with vile creatures who thrive in the dark. Moon heard about the dangerous bog and decided to come to earth to see how bad things really were. She wore her black cloak so nothing could be seen of her at all. She stood next to the bog, with the stars trying to give some light. The peaty water was lapping round her feet, the darkness closed in upon her, and she was truly afraid.

Moon took little steps across the tussocks; she could feel the marsh sucking at her feet, and her cloak was wet and dragging her down. She slipped and her cloak fell over her terrified face, and she tried to hold on to a bramble but it cut into her wrists.

Moon heard a pitiful sound, the sound of a man who has lost his way and is going to slip into the hideous bog. Moon struggled and struggled until she could put back her cape and her light shone across the marsh to light the man on his way.

The creatures of the bog tugged at the terrified Moon and dragged her to the depths, and put a heavy stone on top of her. Time passed and the people became concerned that the Moon had not returned to the sky, and no one, not even the wise woman, seemed to know where Moon was. Then the man recalled how Moon had helped him when he was lost in the bog, and he was certain that Moon was in trouble.

The wise woman at the mill told the villagers to put stones in their mouths and hold hazel twigs, and to go to the bog, just at twilight. A group of

## Moon Calendar

There are calendars that illustrate all the phases of the moon for a year, showing the moon in silver on a deep blue sky. Make one for yourself for a month, either using silver paper or a silver pen on dark-blue paper. Meditate on your picture and the moon rhythm of the month. Allow it to help you find your own rhythm of life, and light a candle for your maiden, mother, or crone, at new moon, full moon or old moon.

villagers did just that, and were very frightened. The bog creatures moaned and pulled at them. The Moon was nowhere to be seen, but they saw the big stone and a flickering light. The bravest among them moved the stone, and for a second saw the bright cold face. The people had to close their eyes, and when they opened them again, there was the Full Moon, back in the Sky; she was smiling at them and they walked home by her silvery light. The moon had not forgotten

them, and they remembered her, and the wicked bog creatures were never the same again. (After Alida Gersie)

Read through this story and think about the different characters – the bog creatures, Moon, the villagers, the lost man and the wise woman. If you were going to make a play of this story, which of the characters would you choose to play? Rewrite the story from that character's point of view.

Find a group of people who could work together on the story and make it into a play. Make masks for your characters and experiment with different ideas. Try telling the story through movement and dance, with lengths of colourful material. Try playing different characters and see if you learn more about yourself and more about the story.

O Mighty goddess of us all
Giver of all fruitfulness
Bring us fruit and grain
flocks and herds
And children to the tribe
That we be mighty

# Sun

At first I did ADORE
a twinkling star,
But now I worship a
CELESTIAL sun

*Two Gentlemen of Verona, 2.vi.10*

Sun energy, like fire energy, is something we usually look forward to. In summer the sun leads us to celebrate the great outdoors. Although it is the time for harvest for farming communities, others pilgrimage to the sunny beach.

In ancient times the permanent loss of the sun in winter was the greatest fear. Would the sun come back again? Festivals of light in diverse cultures were designed to assist the sun's return. Bonfire night is an old pagan sun festival upon which a more modern 'sacrifice' has been imposed. Yuletide is an archaic December festival with candles and bonfires to celebrate the sun. Sun rituals are rarely led by goddesses but when they are, they are very powerful.

# GODDESSES & THE *Sun*

Sun goddesses are all-powerful and are great rulers, who are usually benign. Sun goddesses are frequently associated with the birth-to-death life cycle. They are usually celebrated in midwinter, with bonfires and rich colours.

Sun goddesses are honoured at sunrise and sunset, and when the sun's energy is needed for the crops to grow and flourish. Sunflowers are wonderful symbols of the sun: they tower above the fields and are used at many Mediterranean weddings.

The sun goddess Saule is the great goddess of the Baltic people. She *is* the sun and the weaver of the sky. Like the goddess Freya she is associated with amber, and she guards children and orphans. She is associated with household crafts – weaving, spinning and laundering. She is also a goddess who sings and dances. The following story beautifully describes her summer celebrations:

*Saule was worshipped each day when her people would bow to the east to greet Mother Sun. But she was especially honoured on the summer solstice, Ligo,*
*when she rose, crowned with a braid of red fern blossoms to dance on the hilltops in her silver shoes. At that moment, people dived into east-flowing streams to bathe themselves in her light. All the women donned similar braided wreaths and walked through the fields, singing goddess songs, or* daina. *Finally, they gathered around bonfires and sang the night away.*

(Monaghan, 2000)

Saule reminds us to celebrate, even in the darkest times, and to wear colourful clothes and bright jewellery.

The goddess Han was known as Black of Darkness, and was a primordial goddess of several Native American tribes. The god Skan divided her in half so that one half became the night and the other half became the day. A number of other tribes also have sun deities that are linked with their moon counterparts. For example, the Fox Moon goddess is beneficent and does not cause harm like her partner the sun god.

The Greenland sun goddess from the Arctic had a lover whom she met

Saule, the sun goddess of the Baltic.

by night, so did not know who he was.
One night she marked him with soot
in order to discover his identity. She
was shocked to find out that he was
her brother, Moon. She escaped
carrying her torch, and Moon followed
her. They spend their time following
each other across the sky.

Surya is a sun goddess from India,
daughter and wife of the sun god, and
is said to be a swan maiden, which
gives her an association with wild
birds. The swan motif occurs widely in
northern Europe, the Far East and
elsewhere. Swan maidens turned into
beautiful human maidens to bathe and
then resumed their feather cloaks,
unless captured by a 'handsome
prince'. The story is enacted in the
ballet of *Swan Lake*. One interpretation
is that an agricultural deity is stealing
the 'day mist', and when the swans fly
away it is the end of summer.

The Slavic firebird goddess is also
a sun goddess who is linked with wild
birds. She is said to be the mother
of all birds as well as the hearth. Like
the swan symbol, the firebird motif
appears in many cultures.

# Sophia

Sophia is the divine spark in every human being: she is wisdom and knowledge, right-thinking and caution. She is a solar symbol in Gnostic philosophy, and is referred to in the Old Testament, where she teaches sound judgement and political wisdom.

Sophia is the embodiment of the Holy Spirit and, according to some traditions, she co-created the angels, the world, and was the partner of Jehovah. She can be found in the Jewish and Christian traditions in which she is described as a Tree of Life and it is said that 'all her paths are peace'. Sophia is a paradox: she is elevated as a female divinity, but her roles appear to be very closely defined. She is a deity of cognition rather than feelings. In the following extract from the Old Testament, prudence is emphasized, as is 'correct thinking' and 'correct speech':

*All the words of my mouth are righteous; there is nothing twisted or crooked in them.*
*They are all straight to him who understands and right to those who find knowledge.*

*Take my instruction instead of silver, knowledge rather than choice gold. For wisdom is better than jewels, and all that you may desire cannot compare with her. I, wisdom, dwell in prudence, and I find knowledge and discretion.*

PROVERBS, 8.VIII-XII

Sophia is considered to be a patron of the arts, creativity and practical skills, and can be invoked to help achieve confidence in all these activities. Through her divine light she can be a beacon in the darkness for us. Invoke Sophia when you long for clarity and straightforwardness from others.

*Prize her highly and she will exalt you; she will honour you if you embrace her. She will place on your head a fair garland; she will bestow on you a beautiful crown.*

PROVERBS, 4.VIII-IXe

### A SOPHIA MEDITATION

How often do we long for the right words and regret that we were misunderstood or that something was taken the wrong way. Sit quietly and close your eyes and invoke Sophia to be your guide. See her book in which specific things are written down. Ask Sophia to give you confidence to speak out thoughtfully. Have the confidence to speak for others who perhaps are not articulate. Have the courage to stand tall.

# Ama-terasu-o-mi-kami, Maya & Beiwe

## AMA-TERASU-O-MI-KAMI

Ama-terasu-o-mi-kami is a sun goddess of the Shinto people of Japan. She is one of the few female sun goddesses and is the only female supreme being of a major religion. She is a benign and loving goddess. It is believed that she was created from the menstrual blood of her mother or the left eye of her father. She is considered the ancestor of the Imperial Family in Japan, and her emblem of the rising sun is seen on the Japanese national flag even today.

## THE BEGINNING OF WINTER

Ama-terasu-o-mi-kami had an enormous argument with her brother, the storm god, Susa-no-wo, who was violent and overtly sexual, and who then created mayhem throughout the world. We shall hear more about their fight later in this section. The consequence was that the goddess left the world: she withdrew the sun and turned everything into a long, dark, impenetrable winter. She hid in a cave and ignored the pleadings of many deities. Eight million gods and goddesses beseeched her to come out but she was deaf to them all. The entire world was without light; there was never-ending darkness.

Then Ame-no-uzume, goddess of laughter and ceremonies, who was a shaman and magic ancestor of the clan of chieftains, decided that she had to do something. She overturned a washtub as a platform, and started to sing and dance, screaming lewd remarks. She then started to remove her clothes as she danced wildly, so much so that all the rest of the deities shouted with amusement and glee. Ama-terasu-o-mi-kami began to get curious and eventually peeped through a crack in the cave. The deities placed a mirror there and she looked at herself and saw her beauty for the very first time. While she was distracted, the other deities put in place the 'rope of no return' so that she could never return to the cave. The sun returned to warm the earth, and at last there was an end to the darkness. And now the sun only disappears at night, to return again the next morning.

Ama-terasu-o-mi-kami is celebrated at a festival in early April. She taught people food production, and how to raise silk-worms. Women with young babies invoke her to ensure a plentiful supply of milk. Ama-terasu-o-mi-kami's symbol is a mirror.

## THE SUN DANCE

The Great Plains Indians of North America have an annual festival at which they perform the sun dance, which is considered their most important ritual. At the end of the eight-day celebration they build a symbolic shelter, which represents the home of all humans. The central pole represents the distance between earth and heaven, and it is decorated with symbols of the elements. The warriors, who have pledged themselves to the sun, lead the dance around the pole. Other Native American tribes have a much gorier version of this dance, where they are attached by ropes which are skewered under their pectoral and shoulder muscles (Dixon Kennedy 1996), which then becomes a ritual torture. However the Plains Indian forbade the shedding of blood. Finally in the dance there are invocations to Father Sun and Mother Earth. Morning Star, the spirit of fertility, is called upon to bless the participants.

## MAYA

Maya, who is revered by Buddhists and Hindus in India, is a goddess of illusion with many manifestations, including the sun and daylight, creativity, water and the sea. She is also worshipped in Nepal, Tibet and the Himalayas as the goddess who gives both life and the desire for life. She is sometimes called The Mother of Creation. She is connected with witchcraft and magic. Many of her images are connected with the sun and sunlight, she 'throws light on something' or 'lights up ideas'. However she is also transitory in her association with illusion and delusion.

Maya can assist us when we are muddled, or at a crossroads in our lives, when we do not know which way to turn and our lives feel chaotic. If you long for an instant solution

*Give me clarity in my chaos, and the patience to understand the chaos of others. Let me not have fear because I do not understand.*

and so may panic and make the wrong decision, light a candle and think about Maya and her many faces. Reflect on your life, and ponder whether you actually need to do something or whether it is possible to wait and see if a solution will come to you. Maya can help us understand how we get trapped in 'illusions' about what we want to do with our lives. If we are trapped in an illusory life then we avoid the actual choices that are possible for us. Maya, like Sophia, helps us to be clear.

## BEIWE

Beiwe is a Scandinavian sun goddess who brings fertility to all plants and animals. She is especially associated with reindeer, and it is believed that she travels through the sky every spring with her daughter, Beiwe-Neida, in an enclosure made of reindeer antlers. Beiwe brings the greenness to the Arctic spring and the light to the landscape after the harsh winters dominated by the snow. At first

light, butter is smeared on doors as sacred food for Beiwe. White female animals are sacrificed to her at solstice time. The cooked pieces of flesh were pierced by a stick, which was then bent into a circle and attached with coloured ribbons.

### BEIWE'S GIFT

Beiwe is one of the few goddesses invoked for the relief of mental ill-health and as such is a possible patron of those working with people with mental disorders. She is invoked to 'aid those who are insane'. There is

undoubtedly a high incidence of depression in Northern Scandinavia, where there is an absence of light for up to twenty two hours a day. There is a reality to the feeling of being more optimistic when there is a 'ray of sunshine'; perhaps one reason for the traditional lighting of bonfires in winter is to create warmth and light.

## A MEDITATION FOR MENTAL ILL-HEALTH

These thoughts are for people with mental ill-health, perhaps a member of our family, a close friend or the people with whom we work. The thoughts are also for us when we feel burdened, worried or perplexed as we try to understand these complex phenomena. 'Lunacy' is symbolically associated with the moon and the shadows, and dark winter can cause seasonal depression: let us evoke the goddess to illuminate the situation.

Sit comfortably in order to create some pictures in your mind's eye, which later you will paint or draw. Close your eyes and think about winter – endless cold and the dark

winter of the north. Imagine living with a brief episode of light each day, less than a couple of hours, and that being grey rather than truly light. Now think about the coming of spring: it is getting a little lighter, and a tiny shoot of green can be seen. The green and the light increase and suddenly we see Beiwe, goddess of the sun, riding through the sky with her daughter in the deer-antler enclosure. Reindeer, so important for survival, provide meat and milk, skins and horns. Think about what is important for your survival. Do you feel more burdened at certain times of the year? Think about the seasons, the cycle of the year, and know that spring will come again after winter's darkness.

Open your eyes and think about the brief journey that you have made from darkness to light, from winter to the first shoots of spring, from the empty landscape to the image of Beiwe riding across the sky in spring sunlight. Create a picture, to depict this journey from winter into spring. Remember that life always moves on, and light follows the darkness as daybreak follows night.

# Olwen

Olwen is a Welsh sun goddess who appears in the Arthurian legends. She is called Leaving White Footprints because at every step she took, a white trefoil grew. She is also called White Lady of the Day, Golden Wheel and the Golden Wheel of Summer, with all its brightly coloured flowers.

Olwen's golden wheel is the opposite of the silver wheel of Arianrhod, and evokes Yeats' lines "The silver apples of the moon, The golden apples of the sun."

*She came in wearing a flaming-red silk robe with reddish-gold torc studded with precious stones and red gems about her neck. Her hair was yellower than the flowers of the broom; her skin whiter than the foam of a wave, her palms and fingers whiter than the bloom of the marsh trefoil amidst the sounds of a gushing spring. Neither the eye of a mewed hawk nor the eye of a thrice-mewed falcon was brighter than her own. Her breasts were whiter than a swan's; her cheeks redder than fox-glove; whoever saw her was filled with love of her. Four white clovers would spring up in her track wherever she went. Because of this she was called Olwen, 'White Track'.*

(THE MABINOGIAN)

This wonderful description of the Welsh sun goddess Olwen occurs in the Arthurian-related tales, in the story of Arthur's cousin Chullwch who fell in love with Olwen.

Chullwch enlisted King Arthur's help and Arthur gave seven of his men to help him. Olwen's father, the giant, Ysbaddeden, whose name means 'Giant Hawthorn Tree', forbade the marriage. He imposed thirteen tasks on Chullwch for him to complete before the marriage could be consummated. Arthur and his warriors assisted him and after completing the thirteen tasks, Chullwch slew her father. Olwen became his only wife.

The Arthurian legends give us not only epic adventure stories but also vivid stories of the seasons, the elements and the constellations. Let us remember traditional stories from our own cultures, they are our history.

## WHITE FOOTPRINTS

Imagine yourself as Olwen when she is walking in the landscape and flowers follow her footsteps. Lighten your steps and dance a little: what blossoms grow in your footsteps? Remember to keep a spring in your step as you go about your daily routine, especially when you do not feel inspired. Changing your walk will change your feelings and inspiration may come. By seeing white flowers grow in your footprints, you are making your mark.

# SUN GODDESS *Stories* & EXERCISES

The sun goddesses lead us along many varied paths, through our feelings as well as our intellect, through dazzling brightness and golden chariots. They guide us out of the black winter's night into the promise of the light of the spring, a lived journey from darkness to light. Reflect on the sun within us, the divine spark for all of us.

### AMA-TERASU-O-MI-KAMI'S STORY

Ama-terasu-o-mi-kami had a very unpleasant fight with her brother Susa-no-wo. He had murdered her sister Uke-Mochi, a generous food-giving goddess. As a storm god, he was given to excesses and made sexual advances to his sister. He came to heaven to see her, but she grabbed his sword, broke it and flung it to the earth. Three goddesses grew out of the pieces of blade. Uke-Mochi asked her for jewels, which he cracked open with his teeth and turned into gods. He became more and more excited and, like a hurricane, destroyed everything in his path, even piling up faeces under her throne. He threw a flayed horse through the roof of her weaving room, killing one of her

female companions. This induced Ama-terasu-o-mi-kami to disappear into a cave, creating the first winter.

In this story we can visualize the storm that is out of control and remember incidences when we have been terrified by extreme weather.

We find loud thunder, violent gales or hurricanes very frightening. But there is absolutely nothing we can do, except either hide under the blankets until it passes or gaze out of the window at its magnificence.

If our lives are very stormy and the lives of those around us seem out of control, perhaps we can take comfort from the story of the sun goddess, and find a quiet place to be with ourselves. Even if it is a 'safe place' inside our heads, it can help us to take stock of our situation and decide on the right strategy for our future safety. We need to find a way of keeping safe, both for ourselves and for our children.

### REVERING SUN GODDESSES

Even if you have no small garden, you can still plant a sunflower in a window box and enjoy its growth and blossom. You can then hang up the sunflower seedhead to attract birds. Many of the sun goddesses have connections with birds, and looking after the wild birds can be a way of revering the goddess.

### A BIRD OF FREEDOM

When you are walking in the park or countryside, start to collect feathers to make a bird mask. Cut a mask from card, creating the beak from a separate piece of card. Paint or draw layers of overlapping feathers and finish off the mask by sticking your feathers around the outer edges. Wear your bird mask with a piece of brightly coloured material to create your wings. Feel a sense of freedom as you dramatize a story about the firebird. Write down all your ideas and create a play or a dance for yourself whose title is 'Freedom'. You can also do this exercise with your children or your friends, and create a shared sense of freedom.

### ENJOYING THE SUN

Think about the décor in your house. Do you have a space that you could call the sun room? Maybe it is a conservatory where you can sit and enjoy your plants. If your house has dark areas, with little natural sunlight, and you would like to bring in some light, consider lightening your colour schemes – but be careful not to make them too cold. You could use mirrors to reflect light into dull areas, hang a crystal ornament in your window to catch light on its many facets, or hang curtains decorated with sunflowers or suns. Creating a sunny environment can help us to feel more optimistic inside, even in winter. Allow yourself to enjoy warmth and light.

### WHO ARE YOU?

Do you enjoy getting up in the morning to welcome the dawn, to hear the dawn chorus and to walk in the grass before the dew has disappeared? Or do you stay up in the night to hear the owls and bats and watch the blanket of stars shining through a black velvet sky? Are you a day person, a sun person, or are you a night person, a star person? Give yourself time for your day or your night, your birds or your bats, your sun or your stars. And maybe, just sometimes, you could try the opposite way.

# Section 3

## An Introduction to the Journey of Life

Our journey of life takes us from birth to death through various stages of development. As children, we are aware of targets that are set for us. As we become adults, we are conscious of yet more expectations from our parents and friends and from society. Sometimes our journey takes a path that we do not wish to follow, we feel in an alien landscape, or everything has become a helter-skelter.

Life's journey can be explored in many ways through self-improvement or counselling, but let us also try the old ways. The wisdom of the past can be helpful in the present, especially in times of such rapid change. We try to hold on because things are spinning out of control. We are terrified of dying because we have not yet found the secret of living. We long to change the synthetic present, the images that the media tell us are honest and truthful. The triple goddesses and the goddesses of fertility and childbirth, healing and creativity and knowledge can all help us rediscover where we wish to go, and to find a landscape that is meaningful.

In our journey of life we need resting places, stillness where we can just be, the plateaux where we can gaze. Maybe we need to find this stillness before life has finally run away with us. Pause in your journey, and take joy in the pausing. See what is around you and within you. Only then make plans for your new journey.

*I* beseech you LOOK FORWARD on the journey you shall go.

*MEASURE FOR MEASURE, 43.III.61*

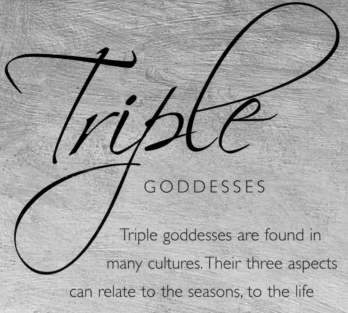

# Triple

## GODDESSES

Triple goddesses are found in many cultures. Their three aspects can relate to the seasons, to the life cycle, to concepts of time or the process of creation. The triple goddesses denote stages of life's journey for women. They can also represent several aspects of our personality, such as the one who inspires, the one who is active, and the one who reflects. Much Western thought is based on either-or dualities: light and dark; young and old; and birth and death. Clusters of three – birth-growth-death, light-twilight-dark – give us process and change. Dualistic thinking takes us to extremes – 'you love me or you don't' – the implications of which we explore later.

*We* FAIRIES that do run
by the triple
Hecate's team.

*A MIDSUMMER NIGHT'S DREAM, 5.1.391*

# GODDESSES & THE *Triple* GODDESSES

The moon's cycle provides us with a clear image of a Triple Goddess, with her phases of new, full and old moon, or maiden, mother and crone. These are believed to be the attributes of the 'Great Goddess' and her power, rather than attributes of three individual goddesses. Other goddesses are described as having three aspects, such as Brigid (see page 20).

Some goddesses are conceived as three individuals, but are nevertheless linked through a single story, such as Persephone, Demeter and Hecate.

Brigid is also known as Bride, who is the maiden, Brig the warrior mother, and Brigid the healer. Monaghan (2000) suggests that she is a triune goddess of smithcraft, poetry and healing, all linked by the symbol of fire, rather than the life cycle. However, we know that Brigid is also associated with milk and is pictured with a cow and a milking stool, therefore we cannot ignore her mother aspect. This would give us Bride the maiden, Brigid the nurturing mother and Brigid the healer crone.

It is believed that three Marys were at the crucifixion. Two of them were at the resurrection: when they went with spices to the tomb of Jesus and found it empty (Luke 14. v1-10). The theme of three Marys recurs in the Cornish eleventh-century Mystery Cycle, where the three Marys are Mary the Mother of Jesus, Mary the Mother of James the Less, and Mary Magdalene.

In Saintes-Maries-de-la-Mer, in the Camargue in Southern France, a local legend relates that three of the Marys sailed in a boat without sails from Palestine together with Black Sara (see page 46). When St Sara is celebrated, especially by Roma gypsies, the statues are carried into the sea escorted by men on horseback, and the sea is blessed. Although many Biblical texts are ambiguous and there could have been anything from two to four Marys, the traditional Triple Goddess already established across Europe appears to be the context in which to place the legend of the three Marys of Camargue.

The Navaho goddess Estanatlehi, or Changing Woman, goddess of all fertility and sterility, is not usually considered a Triple Goddess. However, her capacity to change forms at will brings her into this category. Her name means 'Self-renewing One' and she is believed to be able to change from child to young woman to old woman when she chooses. Her capacity for renewal links her with the seasons.

NOW THERE STOOD BY THE CROSS OF JESUS HIS MOTHER, HIS MOTHER'S SISTER, MARY THE WIFE OF CLEOPHAS, AND MARY MAGDALENE.

(JOHN, 19.v.25)

The story goes that when Estanatlehi gave birth to twins, they grew into young adult males in just eight days. They obtained their father's magic weapons and made sure that no monsters were left on the earth, but the earth had fewer and fewer people. Estanatlehi brushed the dust from her breasts. Her right breast yielded white flour and her left breast gave yellow meal, and she mixed the flour and meal with water to form a paste. Out of the paste she created a man and a woman, who reproduced in plenty for the next few days, so there were enough people to create the four clans of the Navaho people. Estanatlehi went on creating humans from the dust of her nipples, thus making even more clans. The women of these clans became famous for their nipples.

Estanatlehi shows us that it is possible to find new ways of being when we feel stuck in roles or relationships. We are able to change. She has a special relationship with fertility, so meditate upon her when you are thinking about the next generation.

# Demeter, Persephone & Hecate

Demeter, Persephone and Hecate are all goddesses in their own right and Hecate herself is sometimes known as Triple Hecate because of her ability to walk between the seen and unseen worlds and to occupy the space between them. She carries a torch that illuminates the shadows.

It was Hecate the crone who saw the abduction of Demeter's daughter, Persephone, while mother and daughter were picking flowers in the meadow. Hades, god of the underworld, abducted Persephone and took her to his realm to be his bride. On hearing Persephone's screams, Hecate went to tell Demeter, who was already grieving for her lost daughter.

When Demeter could not find Persephone, she sank deeper and deeper into her grief, and the once fertile earth became dry and barren. The gods said that Persephone could return to the earth if she ate nothing in the underworld, but Hades gave her a pomegranate seed, which she ate, so she was committed to stay with him. Eventually a compromise

was reached and Persephone returned to her mother for nine months of the year but had to spend the remaining three months with Hades. The earth blossomed once again and became fertile, and remains so except during the winter months when Persephone returns to Hades under the earth.

This Triple Goddess myth reminds us of the natural cycles of life and that once winter has come, spring will follow. It is a story of the crops and the harvest and the rhythms of the seasons. In the shrines of Demeter only fresh crops are permitted as offerings: the wheat and not the bread, the honey and not the cake, the wool and not the cloth.

Many of us who live in cities have lost touch with the cycle of the seasons and we no longer mark the year with seasonal rituals and celebrations.Now we have freezers and supermarkets, we no longer eat according to the seasons and cheap travel allows us to enjoy warm weather all the year round. Let us rediscover the rituals of the seasons.

## A MEDITATION ON THE CYCLE OF THE SEASONS

Sit and reflect on the traditional seasons: the changing landscape; the fertility and growth of spring, the harvest of autumn and the barrenness of winter. Think about how you could acknowledge the changing seasons and the transitions between them, perhaps by cooking seasonal ritual feasts to share with family and friends. Find and keep some symbol of the seasons as a marker of the natural rhythms of the earth. Whatever your environment, acknowledge the cycle of the seasons and their rhythm.

# Morrigan, Norns & Muses

GODDESSES

## THE MORRIGAN

The Morrigan, the Great Queen of the Celts, is primarily a war goddess. She has three aspects, Macha, Badb and Nemain, who are considered to be the three aspects of the moon (waxing, full and waning) or maiden, mother, crone; or the three mothers.

There are several versions of her story; some people say that Morrigan is one of the triune goddesses, others that Morrigan is the collective word for the three. However, we can be assured that the tales and groupings have gone through various transformations since their archaic past, giving us a rich tapestry.

Some stories associate or interchange Morgan Le Faye with Morrigan, who is said to have been King Arthur's half-sister. Her son Mordred succeeded Arthur, as his sister's son. Some tales suggest that there was an incestuous seduction of Arthur by Morgan but this is likely to be a later debasement of the original story. Morgan was said to have learnt magic from Merlin; she was believed to use magic to win her battles. She was linked with healing water and is associated with rivers, where she washes the warriors' armour.

### MACHA

Morrigan in the aspect of Macha is the goddess of slaughter in war and on the battlefield; the heads that are cut off are known as 'Macha's acorn crop'. She has her own threefold aspect as athlete, wife and mother, and red warrior. The men of Ulster suffered Macha's curse when her mortal husband had forced her to run a race against the horses of the king, although she was pregnant. She won the race and then died, having given birth to twins, and she cursed the men of Ulster, saying that whenever they were in danger they would suffer the pangs of childbirth for five days and four nights, and it would continue for nine times nine generations. The hooded crow is one of her transformations.

### BADB

Badb also presides over the battles and is said to have red webbed feet. She appears after dark and washes all the warriors' blood-stained clothing. Other tales describe her as a giantess who stands astride the river while she washes the armour and clothing of those who will die, and the river flows red until she has finished. She can appear as a wolf or bear or young cow, but usually, like Macha, she appears as a hooded crow, feeding off the carrion of the battlefield. Her name means 'scald-crow'.

### NEMAIN
Nemain is also a powerful war aspect of the Morrigan. Nemain's name is translated as 'the venomous one', 'panic' or 'frenzy'. She is believed to provoke warriors to madness during battle. She is linked to the British war goddess Nemetona, who is also a goddess of the sacred groves.

### SYMBOLS OF THE MORRIGAN
The Morrigan, as an individual or as a triune goddess, is associated with the hooded crow and the raven. She is a powerful war and battle deity, an ancient goddess of death. In her raven aspect she feeds off carrion on the battlefields. The horns blown before the battle were said to imitate the croaking of the raven as an invocation.

### GIFTS OF THE MORRIGAN
The Morrigan, with their war-like aspects, are reminders to us of our own strength. We do not want to be war-like, we may not believe in wars, but many of us need to reclaim our 'woman as warrior' aspect. It is this energy that allows us to overcome obstacles, to fight symbolic battles where there is injustice and prejudice, and to discover the confidence to be accountable for our actions.

Give me strength to do something rather than allow others to do it. Let me not just follow blindly.

*Let me find new inspirations from the Muses in my creativity and thinking. Let me be challenged by the Wyrds out of my complacency.*

## NORNS

The Three Norns come from Nordic, Anglo-Saxon and Germanic traditions; they are also known as the three Fates, and are perhaps best known to us as The Three Wyrds. They appear in Shakespeare's play *Macbeth*, where they are also linked with Hecate

*Great business must*
*be wrought ere noon,*
*Upon the corner of the moon.*
(*MACBETH*, 3.v.22-23).

The sisters' chant and dance in the play also emphasizes the magical numbers three, and three times three, as we find later with the Muses.

*The Weird Sisters, hand in hand,*
*Posters of the sea and land,*
*Thus do go, about, about;*
*Thrice to thine, and thrice to mine,*
*And thrice again, to make up nine.*
*Peace! The charm's wound up.*
MACBETH, I.III.31-36

The names of the Norns are Urd (or Wyrd), who looks backward to the past; Verdandi, who looks out at the present; and Skuld, who is veiled and holds the future in her power. Urd and Verdandi are believed to weave the web of life and the fate of every living person and creature (their names also mean destiny and necessity), and Skuld breaks the thread when we die (her name also means 'being'). It puts the expression 'her life is hanging by a thread' into a mythic context, and may be the source of such phrases as 'just hang in there', for example.

The Wyrd Sisters are the guardians of Yggdrasil, the World Tree, and they keep the tree watered because all life, including the universe itself, depends upon it staying alive. The sisters collect water from the nearby spring, well or

fountain called Urd and sprinkle it on this legendary ash tree – truly a source of healing water that is linked with the past. Perhaps Urd also represents the healing of past events in order to move into the present. It is thought that as the eldest sister she could have existed as a single goddess before becoming a Triple Goddess with her two Wyrd Sisters.

The Wyrd Sisters keep us in touch with the whole of life: the past, present and future, and remind us how much of it may be out of our hands. If we have a troubled family or have had a traumatic bereavement, we may dwell too much in the past. We need to be able to move on and the 'passage of life' of these three sisters can help us do that. The Wyrd Sisters also tell us about the wisdom of older women.

## MUSES

The three Grecian Muses are the goddesses of the arts and sciences, intelligence and all creativity. Again, their continued fame is assured by two of Shakespeare's best-known lines, spoken by the Chorus in the play *Henry V:*

*O for a Muse of fire, that would ascend*
*The brightest heaven of invention,*
*A kingdom for a stage, princes to act,*
*And monarchs to behold the swelling*
*    scene!*

(HENRY V, PROLOGUE 1-4)

Interestingly, Shakespeare invokes a
Muse for imagination in order to tell
his epic, emphasizing his connection
with ancient mythology. He refers to
the Muses again in *A Midsummer
Night's Dream*: 'The thrice three Muses
mourning for the death of Learning' –
a contemporary interest, considering
concerns over the decrease in literacy.

The Muses vary in number, name
and function depending on their
location. The three Muses born on
Mount Helicon are called Aoede,
Melete and Mneme; they offer
inspiration for singing, practising and
memorizing, which are three
important linked functions. In Athens
there are nine Muses: Thalia and
Melpomene, who represent comedy
and tragedy, each wearing a mask and
wreaths; Terpsichore who inspires the
dance; the flute-playing Euterpe the
lyric; Polymnia composes and mimics,
Erato and Calliope create epic and
love poetry respectively; Urania is
goddess of astronomy and Clio ruler
of history.

The Muses are invoked for creative
thought, whether in the arts or the
sciences. Indeed, a Muse will assist us
in forming a hypothesis as we take a
leap of imagination before we try to
prove a new scientific truth. By
grouping the Muses in threes, which is
how they are often sculpted, we can
focus on the process rather than
restricting ourselves to an either/or
choice as we discussed earlier.

# Shakti

Shakti as a Triple Goddess offers us an integration of the light and dark forces, which we can use to create but also to destroy. We can journey into the light and also into the dark. Like the Muses, Shakti can inspire creativity, especially poetry. Shakti can give us energy in our lives.

Shakti is an all-encompassing goddess from India. She is one of the primordial deities and her name means 'power'. All power emanated from her and through her, and she integrates sexual and spiritual energy. Many of the male deities had their personal *shakti*, the force that energized them in spirit, life and sex. There are many pictures showing the goddess lying on the god in an act of divine sexual union.

As a Triple Goddess Shakti brings together Sarasvati, Lakshmi and Kali. Sarasvati is The Flowering One, the goddess of knowledge, whose influence eventually spread to all the arts and creativity. Her shrine is placed in libraries and decorated with flowers. She is also a river goddess associated with fertility and prosperity.

Lakshmi is a goddess of fertility and abundance and she is invoked for prosperity – her head appears on coins. She is revered as a protector of the body and of children. Holy basil, grown near houses and temples, is sacred to her, as are cows. Just as Sarasvati is the river goddess, a personification of the River Sarasvati, Lakshmi is said to have risen from the churning of the ocean at the beginning of time. As with Demeter, her offerings are presented in their natural state – baskets of unhusked rice or seedlings growing in a pot– which associates her with the earth and fertility.

Kali is often portrayed as a devouring goddess of death, but she is also the symbol of eternal time: she does not just destroy life, she also gives it. She is invoked to protect the crops and harvest and to guard against smallpox and cholera. Certain bands of criminals even attribute their failure to their lack of devotion to her. Kali can represent unbridled destruction. She is portrayed bare-breasted, with her hair loose and her tongue hanging out.

## INVOCATION FOR SHAKTI

Shakti allow me to experience my darkness and not be afraid. Let me meet Kali and journey from dark into light. Sarasvati help me to blossom and flower and discover my creativity, and Lakshmi protect me and let me find abundance. Shakti accompany my journey through darkness and help me to believe that I will see light again. When all seems lost reassure me that I will feel creative once more.

# TRIPLE GODDESS *Stories* & EXERCISES

When you reflect on the triple goddess, think about where you are on life's journey, as maiden, mother or crone, and ask yourself if you are content. Our society values the beauty of youth, and motherhood can continue into our sixties. Of all life's stages, it seems to be the crone that we fear most. Yet with age comes wisdom: it is a time to reflect and to change direction if we choose.

One aspect of the crone is grandmotherhood, and the following piece, written by a boy of eight, illustrates this very important stage:

*A grandmother is a woman who has no children of her own, and therefore she loves the boys and girls of other people. Grandmothers have nothing to do. They have only got to be there. If they take us for a walk they go slowly past beautiful leaves and caterpillars. They never say 'Come along quickly' or 'Hurry up for goodness sake'. They are usually fat but not too fat to tie up our shoe strings. They wear spectacles and sometimes they can take out their teeth. They can answer every question, for instance why dogs hate cats and why God isn't married. When they read to us they never leave anything out and they do not mind if it is always the same story. Everyone should try and have a grandmother 'specially those who have no television. Grandmothers are the only grown-ups who always have time.*

(IN JENNINGS, 1999)

LET GO OF THE PAST AND SING
ENJOY THE PRESENT AND PLAY
LOOK FORWARD TO THE FUTURE
AND DANCE

## TRIPLE GODDESS MEDITATION

You can do this exercise at any age and choose which aspect of the triple goddess you wish to focus on as a dominant image. Sit quietly, close your eyes and call to mind one of the Triple Goddesses we have met in the preceding pages. Decide which quality in your life you want to strengthen: maybe it is wisdom or stillness or adventurous energy. Focus on the goddess that has this energy and breathe in the quality for yourself. If you feel you are entering the older stage of life, use this exercise to find a new direction of energy and adventure.

## ELDER BLOSSOMS

People in their elder years often feel that they have to work because their pension is inadequate and they want to help their children and grand-children and to save up in case of future difficulties. Pressure continues throughout their lives and there is no time to stand and pause. Perhaps we need to take stock. Maybe we are filling up our time because it is too painful to stop and reflect. Look at the

Mandala exercise in the section on Creativity and Knowledge and see where your fears are located. Maybe you can look again at your skills and creativity and make room for change. Remember that as crone and elder you are unique!

### LETTING GO OF THE PAST

The Triple Goddess can help us to move on with our lives and not get stuck in an unhelpful past. We all have unresolved issues from childhood or young adulthood, some of them extreme, which may need therapeutic intervention. Artistic therapies such as dramatherapy and playtherapy can, for some people, be more helpful than 'talking therapy'. However we can also help ourselves move forward. The Triple Goddesses who represent past, present and future, such as the Norns, can assist this process.

### WRITING TO THE PAST

Our past, our history, is important, for it creates our foundations. A shaky past can make us feel uncertain and confused about our identity. If we need a guide, it may be that we can find one in a goddess, or we may find support from a play or dramatherapist.

Write a letter to your past, remembering the good times and the bad, the things that were special as well as the things that were unhelpful. End your letter by saying goodbye to the things that hindered you and to the people that hurt you. Take the blessed times into your present to keep you strong. Good memories are important when life become difficult.

When you have written your letter, you may want to decorate it. You may want to read it several times before you decide what to do next, so place it in an envelope with the date on, and keep it safe. You may feel a sense of relief after this exercise. Once you have established the positive things in the present, you may want to burn the letter. If so, do so in a little ceremony.

# Fertility

## & CHILDBIRTH

With ADORATIONS,
fertile tears,
with groans that
THUNDER love.

*Twelth Night, 1.v.274*

Many years ago, the
fertility of the land was of
great concern and was assured with
ritual. People smoked and salted food,
otherwise they ate seasonally. The fertility
of people was also important. Now,
most food is intensively farmed. And
people's fertility is decreasing. Perhaps
it is time to do some stock-taking about
the fertility of our lives. The seasons of
the earth give us a natural rhythm by
which we can lead our lives. Contact
with the earth can be a healing activity,
even if we plant one tub of flowers.
We can bake bread once in a while
and experience real home baking. And
let us break bread with our friends.

# GODDESSES OF *Fertility* & CHILDBIRTH

Goddesses have been associated with fertility in all its aspects since ancient times. The Great Mothers were earth goddesses on whom it was believed that all fertility depended. The earth is often still considered female, and is frequently called 'mother earth'. The fertility of the earth is often dependent on women, as we saw with Inanna (see page 72) and with Demeter (see page 116).

### GAIA

The Greek goddess Gaia is a supreme example of a primordial goddess who is just called 'Earth'. She came out of the formlessness and the chaos before anything had existence. Gaia then created everything: the land, the sky, the other deities and the human race. 'All producing and all nourishing', she had many, many children. She gave birth to the Titans, the first race on the earth, and produced deities and monsters alike, as well as populating the earth with countless creatures.

Gaia is venerated at her shrines and at fissures and holes in the earth that are dedicated to her. She is usually given offerings of barley and honey cakes. She is honoured in modern times across Europe as a possible saviour of the earth during times of pillage and looting.

### ARUNDHATI

In India, the goddess Arundhati is the creator of life; she gave birth to all the divisions of the land. She is also one of the stars in Ursa Major. Her name means 'fidelity', so she is invoked at

marriage ceremonies. She stands on a lotus leaf, floating on the water. Find her star 'Alkor' in the sky and reflect on her relevance to your life. Are you faithful to yourself, your philosophy? Allow the word fidelity (truth) to have meaning in your life.

### THISBE

Thisbe is best remembered as a character in *A Midsummer Night's Dream,* by Shakespeare. Pyramus and Thisbe are separated by their fathers. After a series of misadventures, Pyramus mistakenly thinks Thisbe has been killed, so he kills himself. When Thisbe realizes Pyramus is dead, she kills herself. This links with fertility because the story concerns the despair of those who realize they will have no heirs. The tragedy of families being united through death rather than through life is common in myth.

In Greek mythology, Thisbe is one of the clusters of nymphs who are associated with particular places. She is an earth and nature spirit and is the guardian of the town named after her, south of Mount Helicon.

# Maia

When we celebrate May Day or the spring festival of Beltane, we are also honouring the Greek and Roman goddess Maia. As goddess of nature and fertility, love and sexuality, her rites are celebrated on 1 May, when spring brings the blossoms to the trees and the birds to nest.

Although Christianized as a day dedicated to Mary, mother of Jesus, and sometimes referred to as Mary Queen of the flowers, May Day has very ancient roots, for the fertility of both the earth and of people. Rituals associated with the Green Goddess and the Green Man are still celebrated in rural areas in England on May Day and the blooming of the may bushes is a marker for the turning of the seasons. May or hawthorn blossom must not be brought into the house as it is unlucky.

The month of May is the start of the Celtic summer season, with its outdoor tasks and celebrations. Early summer flowers transform the landscape and May is often a month when we can look around us and be thankful for the abundance and fruitfulness of the landscape.

Although Maia is the Roman goddess of the warmth of spring, including sexual heat, she is also thought of as a grandmother and midwife, so she has multiple roles that are associated with fertility.

Maia is also associated with the Roman goddess Ops, known as The Lady Bountiful, a phrase that expresses the abundant gifts of an earth mother. Ops is a protector of everything associated with agriculture and the fertility of the crops, as well as being a guardian of newborn infants.

Another Roman goddess, Bona Dea, is also worshipped on 1 May and is linked with Maia. She is an earth mother with a serpent symbol, and a following that is restricted to women, although men could benefit from her healing. As well as being a patron of health and healing, she is also skilled at averting earthquakes. Ops, Bona Dea and Maia are linked to the goddess Fauna, who is said to personify the earth and its fertility.

## A MAY DAY CELEBRATION FOR FAMILY AND FRIENDS

Maia is about celebration and May Day is a day for joyousness and playfulness. It is a time to dance a May dance. Make a May cake with blossom and sand. Put blossoms from fruit or ornamental trees into the bottom of an old cake tin, fill it up with damp sand or earth and carefully turn it out for a beautiful blossomed May cake. Let us buy a spring dress or a flowered hat.

# Atargatis, Parvati & Uks Akka

## ATARGATIS

Atargatis is an ancient fertility goddess who created the whole of the world. She is probably Syrian or Aramaic, and is thought to be linked with Ishtar, Anat and Astarte. She is usually represented as a mermaid, with the tail of a fish and

the body of a woman, and her followers refuse to eat fish out of respect for her.

There are various stories about her origins. One legend tells us that she came to earth in an egg; the egg landed in the River Euphrates and Atargatis was born in her mermaid form. Another story suggests that she was the mermaid transformed from the body and spirit of a girl who had thrown herself into the river.

Monaghan (2000) tells us that Atargatis was very beautiful and also wise. She was cursed by a jealous rival, who made her fall in love with a handsome young man. She became pregnant and gave birth to a goddess-daughter named Semiramis, whom she left in the wilderness to be cared for by doves. Doves therefore became sacred to her and her followers did not eat them.

### THE WORSHIP OF ATARGATIS

The worship of Atargatis spread throughout Egypt, ancient Palestine, Asia Minor and Greece, where she is represented in various forms. In Greece and Egypt she is depicted with snakes, whereas in Rome she sits on a throne between two lions. She is also linked with Ate, a goddess from Anatolia who rides a lion and carries a sacred dove.

Atargatis is believed to have given rebirth to Jonah. A Babylonian fish god, Jonah is linked with the Jonah who appears in the Old Testament, who was swallowed by a whale. Atargatis also appears as a sea goddess, with a crown of dolphins.

### THE STORY OF THE NINE DAUGHTERS OF ATARGATIS

It was a stormy night and the Phoenician traders looked at the turbulent seas and wondered whether anyone has killed an albatross. They were headed for the Pretannic Isles with cargoes of silks, spices and nutmeg, rough and sweet wines, so popular with the Celts, and assorted dyes, especially the coveted cobalt. They hoped for tin and maybe wool rugs and raw wool bales. The three ships were the single-masted traders, strong and flat, resistant in most weathers. The captain of the largest of the three ships regularly made the run to the Pretannic Isles; he enjoyed Celtic hospitality, especially of his favourite girl, Rigantona, daughter of a local chieftain. Should he stay with her this time? If they made it, of course — the ships were uncomfortable in the heavy silver waters.

## MERMAIDS OF AVALON

There were nine mermaids, daughters of Atargatis, who were escorting the ships on their voyage. The mermaids, confident and adventurous, circled the boats, laughing and singing, daring each other to seduce a sailor, rather looking forward to exploring the Pretannic Isles. Land came in sight and the boats steered up the channel and moored at a quayside. The sailors lept ashore, glad to be on dry land for a few days. The mermaids swam further inland, across the marshy plains toward the ancient isles of Avalon. The sacred apple orchards beckoned the daughters of Atargatis and the sailors started their hard trading and their equally hard drinking.

The mermaids decided to stay in Avalon and the sailors returned home, the captain saying to himself that perhaps next time he will stay. In time the waters around Avalon started to recede, and the daughters of Atargatis remain by the sacred wells and springs as guardians and healers.

(Inspired by Pauline Royce, sacred doll maker, and her tale)

*Diving to the depths of the sea, I can see wondrous coral and floating shapes; looking out across the seascape, the inviting land is calling me.*

*Did I sing when my baby arrived, to open the door into this world?*
*Let me sing now to welcome all children onto this earth.*

### UKS AKKA

Uks Akka is known as 'The Old Lady of the Door'; she welcomes newborn babies from the darkness into the light. She is the goddess of the Saami people of Lapland and lives at the doorway of the tent in order to bless all people who go out or in. She is believed to have the skill to change girl babies into boys. She is one of the daughters of the earth mother Akka, who is also known as Rauni in Sweden, meaning rowan, and the rowan tree is sacred to her. Her father is Ukko, a supreme deity who is also a god of fertility, presiding over a planting festival where men and women couple together in the woods. Uks Akka forms a triad with her sisters, Juks-Akka and Sar-Akka, who are also goddesses of fertility and childbirth.

### SAR-AKKA

Sar-Akka is the goddess who opens the womb for the baby to be born. Wood is chopped outside the birthing tent – this is believed to help her make the opening.

The mother makes offerings to Sar-Akka both before and after the birth. While still in labour she drinks brandy in honour of the goddess and after the birth she eats a specially prepared porridge. The porridge contains three predictive sticks: a white one fortells good luck; a black one predicts death; and a forked one suggests success in life. The future of the

infant is predicted by Sar-Akka by
the position of the sticks.

## JUKS-AKKA

Juks-Akka is also a birthing goddess
but she is only concerned with the
birth of boys. Porridge is made to
honour her after the birth of a boy,
and a tiny bow is placed in the
porridge to ensure that he grows
into a strong hunter.

  The 'open womb – open door'
functions of the Akka goddesses echo
the practice of the Temiars of the
Malaysian rainforest. In the last stages
of childbirth, the midwife not only
calls upon the river and thunder deity,
but also on everyone around, to
'open', so any women nearby sit with
their legs wide apart, and fishing nets,
suitcases and saucepans are all
opened as well.

## PARVATI

Parvati is a great goddess of India and
appears in many guises. She practised
'magical asceticism' to gain the
attention of Shiva, lord of the dance.
They had many disputes about having

children, and Shiva cut the head
off her baby and then, with remorse,
replaced it with the head of an
elephant. The child became the god
Ganesh, a god of good fortune.
Perhaps Parvati's story reminds us

to be clear about whether we
really want children or not, and
whether both parents agree. We
need not feel obligated to reproduce
and we can take joy in the children
of others.

### PARVATI'S GIFTS

Parvati exemplifies single-mindedness: she even prayed sucessfully for her skin colour
to be changed because Shiva thought she was too dark. A powerful goddess, she
cannot always control her anger: it escaped out of her mouth in the form of a lion
when she cursed a guard. We can admire Parvati for her strength and perhaps we
need to be cautious about both her jealousy and her self-effacement.

# Hathor

Hathor is one of the great goddesses of Egypt, with many names and attributes, including The Celestial Cow, Queen of the Earth and Lady of the Cemetery. She is an earth goddess as well as a goddess of the underworld. She is a passionate goddess who can also be destructive.

We usually see Hathor with the face of a cow, with a solar disk between her horns. She is also depicted as a lion, a woman and a tree.

As Mother Goddess, Hathor had seven forms – 'the Hathors' – and she was celebrated on New Year's day at her great Temple at Dendera. Her statue was carried out to catch the rays of the rising sun and then followed an orgiastic party with wine, food and sex. It was a time of celebration of abundance.

Hathor also has her destructive side and was said to have destroyed thousands of people when one of her sons, Ra, said that he was scared of his enemies. She had such a blood lust that in the end Ra was concerned that the human race would be wiped out. He spread red dye over the land and Hathor drank it and became intoxicated and forgot the killing. It is an interesting story to compare with

the similar story of the Egyptian goddess Sekhmet (see page 18).

As Queen of the Underworld, Hathor has control of the dead, and in her seven aspects she nourishes the souls of the newborn infants, as well as those who have died.

Hathor is celebrated in first love, in the rapture and loss of self that happens just once in one's lifetime. She is a very sensory goddess, so music, wine and dance are effective ways of invoking Hathor. Maybe she should be celebrated with others, perhaps special friends, with dancing and singing.

Hathor was revered for thousands of years. If she seems too noisy a goddess for you, think about her sense of enjoyment and her passion. How long is it since you felt passion about a person or a cause? Allow Hathor to bring you fertile ideas when you get stuck, to break through the barrier into new colour, new sounds and fun.

## HATHOR QUESTIONS

Do you feel stuck? Do you long for movement? Which artistic form are you drawn to? Whether it is dancing, singing, painting, gardening or theatre, create something with passion. Allow your passionate self to have expression. Can this guide you in the future? Hathor was celebrated for several thousand years, so what was her essence? Can she help you find creativity and to celebrate for no reason?

Goddesses of fertility and childbirth can help us get in touch with the larger landscape. When we are childless we may long for the infant who never arrives and our situation seems unique to us. Remember that we share it with many.

### FERTILE DIFFICULTIES

There are many stories on themes of fertility and childbirth. Some specifically address the issues of conception and childbirth. Others connect us to the more fertile aspects of our lives as a whole and help us to be more creative in work and play.

When people are childless and their most earnest wish is for a baby, everything else takes second place while they try to change this painful situation. For some people medical intervention is helpful and does result in a take-home baby. For others there is no baby and no explanation for their lack of fertility.

### DIFFICULTIES WITH CONCEPTION

People sometimes allow baby-making to become the only focus of their lives, and may feel desperate. Many of the exercises in previous sections can help reduce stress and anxiety. All of the exercises address issues of slowing down and refocusing our ideas and feelings. There are techniques for creating as well as healing. There are stories for new journeys and landscapes. Choose something that seems right for you now, while you reflect on your situation.

People have been helped to have babies by becoming creative in other ways. Maybe they have created a special garden, or have started cooking in a different way, or have learned to embroider. Many of these activities can be shared by partners. When a couple decide to forget about babies for a while and undertake a creative activity or take a holiday, it is surprising how often a baby is then conceived.

This does not make it easier for those who never conceive and who long for a child. It is important that people are allowed to grieve for the child they will never have and acknowledge the pain before moving on. There will be many decisions to make, but they should not be hurried. Painting, dancing, poetry, stories and music can all be helpful in expressing feelings of grief and sadness and then our journey of reconciliation.

### CREATIVE JOURNEYS

In a land far away there is an ancient green forest with trees that are hundreds of years old. A river runs through the forest, and animals come down to the river bank to drink. The trees meet over the river, creating a green tunnel, and the river is slow-flowing, rippling over the stones and debris and washing against low

branches. The forest is hundreds of years old and trees tower up into the air. Layer upon layer of vegetation in this forest lie undisturbed. The forest holds many secrets that have never been told, and contains stories of many generations. The river flows on, washing away the wounds as it goes.

Read through this story slowly and then sit quietly and reflect on all the images of the forest and the river. Say the chant (below right) to yourself as you trust the forest and the river to help you find a new direction.

CELEBRATIONS FOR CHILDBIRTH
Remember Uks-Akka and her two sisters who assisted with childbirth in Lapland? If you have your baby at home, you have far more control over how you give birth. Many women choose to have babies in birthing pools, with muted lighting and soothing music. If you decide to go to hospital, you can still make the birth setting less high-tech and mechanistic. Find a midwife and doctor who will listen to your concerns, and agree on a birth plan that includes your own

ideas. Once the baby has arrived, it is time for celebration. Firstly, celebrate the mother and all her hard work – she has achieved a miracle and needs all the affirmation she can get. Then celebrate the baby, a new creation in the world. The father can also be celebrated, but this is not his big day – he is the supporter in these events.

Your new baby is already social and longs for your company. Within hours of birth your baby may be smiling, and within a few days may respond to your smile. The drama has begun of the playing between mother and child. It is a play of fun and silliness, of mimicry and testing. It is essential for living and is enjoyable for all concerned.

Playing for life is just that. It is playing for life and health. Whether it is stories, games or make-believe, playing is crucial for our survival and will ensure a fertile future for our children.

SPIRIT OF THE FOREST, HOLD MY STORY
SPIRIT OF THE RIVER, HEAL MY PAIN
SPIRITS OF NATURE, WITNESS MY LIFE

# Healing

We long for good health
but worry about ill health.
We know that anxiety and
pressure increase our discomfort
but we continue to follow stressful
lifestyles. We yearn for contentment, but
the present is never adequate and we
live in the future. It may take a major crisis
for us to take stock and change our lives.
Then each day can seem precious and
we enjoy it as it arises. Life appears to
slow down. Our perspective changes and
our striving for the future is transformed
into a greater contentment with the
present. Perhaps, by taking life a step at
a time, we can find new ways of
appreciating ourselves and those around
us to affirm our health and happiness.

To the most WHOLESOME
physic of thy health-giving air.

*LOVE'S LABOURS LOST, 1.1.236*

GODDESSES & *Healing*

142

GODDESSES

Many goddesses are associated with healing, and their healing waters, trees or shrines have been revered since ancient times. We use them to maintain our health or to bring about healing for ourselves, our friends and our families. Sacred wells and springs, whether dedicated to saints or goddesses, can still be seen today with messages or invocations for well-being. Pieces of material or clothes are tied to trees or bushes, having been first dipped in the water. One Brigid well in Northern Ireland is believed to heal feet, and there are rows of babies' socks tied to the hawthorn bush over the well. The Brigid invocation on the right is very calming.

We light candles at holy shrines for the health and well-being of people dear to us, and make pilgrimages to places of veneration of goddesses and saints. Often these places are sites of multiple worship and are associated with miracles. The very landscape seems to be imbued with healing energy.

The goddess Mella from Zimbabwe is invoked for healing and courage. Mella's father was slowly dying and it seemed that no one could cure him, so she went to the moon goddess for advice. The moon goddess said that she must go to the dangerous Python Healer and he would help her. Although Mella was terrified, she went to the Python Healer's cave to ask for his help. He wrapped himself around her, and she carried him to her father, and he cured him. She carried him back to his cave and he invited her inside, where she saw amazing jewels and riches. Python Healer asked Mella to choose a gift for herself because of her courage and deep love for her father. Mella asked him to choose something and he gave her a necklace with a moon pendant. When Mella became queen, she had a statue carved of Python Healer and placed it in the centre of the village.

Mella's story illustrates selflessness and the overcoming of great fear in order to bring about healing and change. Meditate on this story when you need healing in your life.

In Japan, female shamans are believed to be better healers than male shamans, especially if they also practise divination. Ame-no-sade-yori-hime, known as Heavenly-Net-pulling-hither-Princess was venerated on the island of U-Shima. She reminds us of the strength of women's wisdom. She was also an oracle and acknowledging her powers can help us to find our own voice of wisdom.

The North Star goddess from China, Dou Mou, is revered not only as a healing goddess but also for her connection with education, knowledge, commerce, family, the stars and the planets. She has nine children who were the original rulers of the earth. She is invoked for protection against disease and dangers when travelling. Dou Mou is called the bushel goddess because the North Star constellation is also called the Star-Bushel.

The Hindu goddess Kali, whom we met in the Triple Goddess section as the dark side of Shakti (see page 122), is also an important healing goddess in her own right. She is so strongly associated with death that it is sometimes possible to forget her life-promoting and healing properties: she is part of the whole cycle of life, including death. The Naya peoples make sacrifices to her during smallpox and cholera epidemics. Kali is very powerful when we need to address our fears and overcome them, including the fear of death. Kali can be an extreme goddess and we hear lurid tales of blood sacrifices, so stay calm with her image and realize that she has faced the dangers and can therefore help us to do the same.

BRIGIT OF THE MANTLES, BRIGIT OF THE PEAT HEAP,
BRIGIT OF THE TWINING HAIR, BRIGIT OF THE AUGURY,

BRIGIT OF THE WHITE FEET, BRIGIT OF CALMNESS,
BRIGIT OF THE WHITE PALMS, BRIGIT OF THE KINE.

(CARMICHAEL, 1994)

# Kuan Yin

Kuan Yin is a Bodhisattva, one who in traditional Buddhist thought has acquired great moral and spiritual wisdom, especially one who rejects Nirvana in order to assist suffering mankind. She is sometimes considered to be a folk goddess and to have links with an older goddess tradition.

Above all, Kuan Yin represents mercy and compassion. She protects women and children and keeps them healthy.

Kuan Yin can help us during extreme pain and suffering, as she is believed to listen to every supplication. Indeed the reason that she stays on earth is to alleviate human ill-health. She is also invoked to help gain knowledge and education and to enhance physical prowess.

Kuan Yin is usually depicted in flowing garments, carrying willow to sweep away illness. She has many emblems, including the lotus flower, signifying purity and grace, and a jewelled bowl, which contains healing water. She also has emblematic weapons, including a thunderbolt for killing demons and an axe for dealing with oppressors.

She is associated with sound, and is referred to as The Melodious Voice, which links us to music and voice as a healing medium. She has the capacity to change into any being that is close to the person she is healing. If she is healing a child, she will turn into a child, and will act similarly with any man or woman.

Kuan Yin leads us by her example and hopes that we too will show compassion and understanding. She has infinite patience as we stumble on our journey to spiritual wisdom.

Kuan Yin can help us find serenity, which is perhaps her greatest attribute. Meditating on a picture of a lotus may be the first step toward finding some peace in this turbulent world. Kuan Yin can help us to deal with our rage when we are ready to explode. Meditate on her healing water and see it flowing down the mountain, taking your anger away to the sea. If you can find a statue of Kuan Yin in her open-handed position, her very generosity will help you pause and think again.

## THE HEALING VOICE

Sit quietly and meditate on the voices you hear in your life: those you do not listen to, those which are harsh, and those which command you attention. Listen to your own voice and question whether it is your *real* voice. Maybe your voice needs to heal from hurt. Say something quietly to yourself in a voice that feels real to you. Find or write a poem that expresses your hurt and speak it quietly in your real voice.

# Panacea, Aimed & Die Hexe

## PANACEA

Panacea is the Greek goddess of health and healing. She is the daughter of the patron of physicians, Asklepius, and his healing wife Epione. Panacea has three sisters, including Hygeia, who is a healing goddess, one whose name means 'health'. Hygeia's name was also given to Athena as the guardian of mental ill-health. Another sister is Iaso, whose name means 'recovery', and she is also a goddess of medicine. Panacea's youngest sister is Aigle, who appears to have several manifestations as one of the three Hesperides and other groups in the Greek pantheon. However, like her three sisters, Aigle is also a medicine goddess. She turned herself into a willow tree when she heard the desperate prayers of Orpheus.

We use the word *panacea* or *panakeia* in a context like 'universal panacea', meaning 'all healing' or 'universal remedy' from the Greek words *pan*, meaning 'all' and *akos*, meaning 'remedy.' So in the above phrase, 'universal' is redundant, because *pan* means 'all' or 'universal.' These days it is used more frequently in a social context than in a healing one, and is also heard in public meetings and in parliament.

## AIRMED

Airmed is the Irish goddess of medicine and healing and, like Panacea, she is the daughter of a physician. Her father Dian Cecht is a god of medicine who, together with his daughter, guards the secret well of healing. Airmed is an ancient goddess with supreme skills of herbs and healing lore, witchcraft and curing. She learned her healing knowledge from her brother Miach, who was also a great physician, especially of the nervous system.

A STORY OF HEALING GRIEF

Dian Cecht was extremely jealous of the medical skills of his son Miach and, realizing that his son was a better healer than himself, he killed him. Airmed, grieving, buried her brother with sadness and love, and all the herbs needed for healing grew from his grave. Airmed would pick these herbs and learned how to use them for healing, and like her brother she was able to heal the nervous system. One day when she had all her herbs laid out on her cloak by the grave of her brother, her father came and turned the cloak over so all the herbs were mingled together. Thus, her father told her, the humans will never know the secrets of immortality that might be gained through those herbs.

Some sources say that Airmed also had a sister, Etain, who was another goddess of medicine. She was married to Ogma, the god of eloquence and literature, and she was known as a sun and horse deity.

HEALING WATER

Just as Sulis presided over the healing waters of Bath, so there are many goddesses who are associated with springs, wells and rivers in many parts of the world, as we saw in the

$\mathcal{A}$ncient goddess of healing, let me be true to myself, authentic to others, and acknowledge your ancient lore. Let me find healing.

Elements section on Water. Segeta is the goddess of the healing water at Aquae Segeta, near the River Loire in France; Sequana has a shrine at the headwaters of the River Seine, where she is a goddess of healing; the Griselicae Nymphae live in the healing springs at Basses-Alpes, in Southern France, and are healing water sprites. In Ireland countless healing wells and springs are dedicated to Brigid.

The Carmenae are prophetic nymphs of fountains and springs and are associated with the sacred grove where the Vestal Virgins drew their water. The Therma are Grecian water nymphs of the springs of Apameia, and Diana is called Thermia when she presides over healing springs and waters. Similarly Artemis is called Thermaia when she is goddess of health and healing. Moving away from Western Europe, Ganga is the personification of the Ganges river in India and is the chief river deity, who bestows health over much of the land. Ahurani is a Persian water deity who is linked with healing and prosperity. A daytime goddess, she can only be revered during daylight. Finally Oshun (see page 26) heals with her sweet waters from the head of the Oshun river in her native Nigeria.

## DIE HEXE
Die Hexe, who are of German origin, are a group of healing witches. They are able to weave spells that will cure adults and children. They are also able to control the weather. The Hexe have been adopted by Roma gypsies, who believe in their healing magic and

their ability to influence the natural world. There are 'Hexe doctors' who use ancient formulas to remove spells and curses, and almost always use their skills for white rather than black magic. We talk about 'hexing' someone, or being 'hexed'; the verb means to put a spell on somebody or to be bewitched. As a noun it can mean a witch or a spell.

## CONTEMPORARY 'WITCHES'

The popularization of witch stories on television has meant that we are less in touch with the very primitive earth magic that belonged to the Hexe. People are very apprehensive about anything that sounds like 'witchcraft' and 'black magic', and so prefer their witches with hag-like faces, riding on broomsticks through the night. Otherwise they are young and sexy and usually upset the status quo at school in a rather light and fluffy way. The Harry Potter stories take magic and mystery into a more serious vein; even so there are parents and ministers who do not approve. The Hexe have been persecuted

for hundreds of years of European history, although their knowledge of healing and herbalism is very ancient lore. All old women who healed and delivered babies in rural areas were under suspicion of being witches. If a child was born dead or a crop failed, then the finger of suspicion pointed at the old women. In the play *Macbeth*, Shakespeare was writing in the middle of the witch craze in Europe and was quite brave to have his witches invoke Hecate at a time when popular opinion maintained that all witches were in league with the devil.

Earth rituals like those chanted by the Hexe or witches contain powerful healing energy that follows the rhythm of the seasons and the natural herbs and fruits. It is so strong that we must take care that it stays as a positive force and doesn't go

to the opposite extreme and become destructive. An ancient Hexe cure for children's nightmares is to place the herb rosemary near the bed at night – hang sprigs near the bed for an infant, and place them under the pillow for a teenager or for yourself.

## ELEMENTS OF HEALING

In this section we can see that all the elements can be a part of the healing process. We have talked about healing water and earth rituals, as well as lighting candles for well-being. Many important healing exercises are based on the very air we breathe. Regulating the breath and controlling the inflow of air during meditation and yoga can be deeply healing. By balancing the healing energies of water, earth, fire and air we bring harmony to our lives.

BLESSED BE THE ELEMENTS OF MY BEING
BLESSED BE THE ELEMENTS IN MY BEING
BLESSED BE THE ELEMENTS FOR MY WELL-BEING
BLESSED BE

# Sul

Sul or Sulis is the goddess of health in the city of Bath, England, where the natural hot healing springs, called Aquae Sulis by the Romans, were named after her. The healing powers of the waters of Sulis were famous both in England and across the sea on the European mainland.

Sul's name means 'eye' or 'seeing' in Celtic, and Gimbutas (2001) suggests that her epithet 'Suliviae' means 'twin-sunned', which she describes as a semantic transfer from 'eye to sun'; thus the 'magic regenerating eyes of this goddess were seen as suns'.

Sulis had permanent fires alight at her shrine and the water was always warm, all leading to the opinion that she was a sun as well as a water goddess. However, Sulis was known in

## HEALING MY BODY, HEALING MY SOUL
## HEALING MY SPIRIT, HEALING MY HOME
## GODDESS SUL,
### HELP ME TO HEAL MYSELF

multiple forms in England and the continent and as the triple goddess Suliviae had many similarities to Brigid.

Sul is possibly linked with the earth mother goddess of Silbury Hill in Wiltshire, England, for whom there is a celebration at Candlemas, with a procession to the sacred springs at Suilohead. If this is the case then she is linked with at least three of the four elements.

The Romans adopted Sul when they arrived in southwest England and, after the local people protested at changing her name, a compromise was reached: she was called Sulis Minerva in England and, in Rome, Minerva Medica. Sulis is depicted as a matron in heavy clothes, 'with a hat made out of a bear's head and her foot resting on a fat little owl' according to Monaghan (2000).

Sulis is specifically recognized as a healing goddess throughout Europe rather than as a multiple and varied deity. Her baths at Bath have been beautifully restored, and there are currently plans to open new spring-fed baths: perhaps Sulis is about to recover her healing spa.

## A SULIS INVOCATION

'Sulis cleanse me of my doubt, Sulis heal me from my complacency.' Meditate on Sulis and her healing hot springs to regenerate your love of life. Let Sulis wash away your tears after losses and help you flow in new directions. Listen to the sound of running water or go and sit near a pool and lake and watch the movement of the water. Discover the healing springs or ancient baths near where you live and visit them for contemplation.

Goddesses of healing remind us all to take care of ourselves and not to tolerate an unfulfilling way of life. We need not stay in destructive relationships or continue to feel unwell. Allow the goddesses to help you discover a healing space and a healing journey. Likewise, a small corner in your home can become a sanctuary.

### A HEALING STORY

There is an ancient apple tree with deep, deep roots. Layer upon layer of branches bent with the heavy crop of fruit grows upwards and outwards. A child climbs the tree, nimbly skirting the bees' combs and birds' nests, and she sits aloft, looking out across the landscape. An old woman walks slowly and sits among the roots, leaning her head against the trunk, she quietly

sleeps. The moon comes out and bathes the apples in her silver light and a she-wolf comes out of the forest and stares up at the tree. As dusk approaches the child looks perturbed, and the wolf comes up to the old woman and licks her face.

She continues to sleep contentedly, and the wolf calls the child down from the tree. The little girl is sleepy, and she scrambles down and climbs on to the back of the wolf. The wolf glances at the old woman and then pads back into the forest. (S. JENNINGS 2000)

### HEALING GARDENS IN SMALL SPACES

To create a healing garden it may be enough for you to plant with care some pots with aromatic herbs such as rosemary and thyme, and to arrange some river stones or shells in patterns. You could create the healing shape of the spiral in bricks or stones and plant it with herbs.

Small fruit and berry trees, such as apple or rowan, can be grown in tubs. Choose a tree that is right for you, perhaps from a healing story. Wind chimes made from natural materials will give you healing sounds. Fill a sturdy pottery bowl with water in which you can float petals or candles when the breeze is gentle.

Now you have all the elements in your healing space. This is the place for meditation and quiet reflection, for time out, to read or to make decisions. Share this healing space with others who need to pause in a confusing landscape and encourage birds by adding a small bird feeder.

You can slowly develop your space. The choice of a goddess statue to place in a shrine is a very personal matter; it is a good idea to ask the goddess first. You might try to create one yourself out of clay or find yourself drawn to a specific statue, but make sure it withstands the outdoors. Create a corner niche where you can place flowers and candles, and use it as a focus for your healing meditations.

## LARGER GARDENS

The possibilities are endless if you have a bigger space. You can create an apple orchard or a sacred grove with willows or hazel trees. Start with what is in the garden and add to it, rather than rip out what is already there. You can create wild and orderly spaces, allow habitats for wildlife, and plant aromatic and colourful borders. You may have room for a fountain or small waterfall. Create shapes with stones, plants or driftwood. Connect the elements, ornaments and statues with stones or glass pebbles.

## HEALING SPACES INDOORS

A healing space starts as a quiet area of your home. Maybe it needs to be near a window where you can hang a wind chime and put plants on a sill or a bowl with sand and stone patterns. An oil burner will create healing scents and an indoor water feature will provide water sounds. Take care with naked flames, especially near curtains, but floating candles and oil burners are usually safe. You can create your own goddess shrine. Take time to allow your healing space to evolve. You will intuitively know what is right for it if you give your inner self space to listen.

## HEALING MEDITATION

Sit quietly in your healing space, and reflect on the seasons: the blossoming and the fruiting, then the harvest, the dark winter, and then the blossoming again. The cycle of the seasons creates a natural rhythm through different landscapes; allow it to flow, knowing that good times will come again.

GREATEST MOTHER OF THEM ALL
SEND FRUITFULNESS TO TREES AND PLANTS
ABUNDANT HARVESTS, FLOCKS AND HERDS
AND CHILDREN TO THE TRIBE, THAT THEY BE MIGHTY

# Creativity

## & KNOWLEDGE

Everybody is creative: we may
draw, paint, weave, decorate our
homes or cook. When we are creative,
we use our imagination to transform
something into something else – the
paints into a picture, the ingredients into
a cake. Our knowledge and experience
are the starting points for creativity.
Knowledge is not just stored information,
it is our understanding. Often creativity
helps us make sense of our experience.
If we play music when we feel tense, we
may feel calmer and understand the
stress. The real starting point for
creativity is through our play as children.
Through play we discover our creativity
and understand the world about us.

O any thing, of nothing
first CREATE!
O HEAVY alightness!

ROMEO AND JULIET, 1.1.183

*Creativity*

Many of the goddesses that we have already met in this book are linked with creativity and the arts, with knowledge and education. Some of the Muses described in the last section are linked to specific creative art forms and are portrayed with their appropriate symbols such as a mask, a musical instrument, a scroll or an open book.

When we are seeking inspiration, we may 'muse' on a theme or we 'amuse' our children, or even go to a 'museum'. All these words are derived from the Muses (see page 120) and are now part of both our everyday language and of creative process.

The elements – fire, earth, water and air – give us inspiration in our creativity. Think how many paintings include one or more elements, for example. We often integrate all the elements when we plan our new garden; we have a water feature, wind chimes, lighting and a barbecue. We paint our houses with earth colours or sea pictures and so on.

Some goddesses of the elements are specifically linked with the arts and with creativity. The Tibetan

fire goddess, gLu-maa Ghirdhima, is a dancing goddess who is also associated with music and song, and the Celtic goddess Brigid is the patron of poets. In China there is an embroidery goddess who is a goddess of household matters.

She is known as a needlework deity because of her skills, and young girls learning embroidery invoke her to assist them.

## CREATIVE GIFTS

There are also specific goddesses who are considered to have brought the gifts of knowledge, creativity and therefore education to the world. For example, the Native American goddess Grandmother Spider is believed to have woven the alphabet into being. Saga from Scandinavia is a goddess of arts, knowledge and education. Her name is 'All Knowing' and she is believed to be a patron of both poetry and the telling of stories, especially stories of their history. These days a saga is a long epic story, often of heroic achievement. We use it colloquially to recount an event: 'such a saga'. Perhaps we have re-invented Saga now as a goddess of those people of riper years!

Cailleach Beara is an ancient British goddess of creation, education and knowledge and also of earth and nature, agriculture and families. She

is said to be an old hag and a wise woman, and is known as Old Woman in Ireland and Scotland. She was immensely strong and carried boulders in her apron as she shaped the landscape. She made the rivers flow, she 'let them loose' and 'waved her hammer over the grass', and she had control over the dark months of winter. According to Monaghan (2000), she could endlessly renew her youth: as her countless husbands died of old age, she became young again and found yet another young partner. She had fifty foster-children who created many tribes and nations.

Danu is an Irish Celtic goddess who is known as 'Mother of the Gods' and who is an ancestor of Tuatha De Danaan. The De Danaan are the fourth colonizing people; they came to Ireland many centuries before Christianity. They were bearers of knowledge and light, who overcame the darkness of the Formorii, and brought with them well-developed skills of science and metalworking. Danu is considered to be the goddess of education and knowledge, as well as being associated with the family and the tribes.

### KNOWLEDGE AND LIFE

Pawnee First Woman is a Native American deity who looks after education and knowledge, agriculture and household affairs. She is also is a creator of life. Daughter of Evening Star, she is a teacher who passes her knowledge of the world to the people.

In the early beginnings Pawnee First Woman lived in the heavens where she was born. Her mother taught her many things about the world so that she could pass on this knowledge to the people. She came to earth on a cloud that was driven by a whirlwind. She was able to teach the people about gardening and planting. She taught them how to make an earth lodge. She also taught them how to speak and communicate to others and how to live their lives.

### GIFTS OF THE GODDESS

These goddesses show us how to have a balance between thought and feelings, knowledge and experience. They also emphasize the importance of communication.

# Bast

Bast is an Egyptian goddess of the arts and of healing. She is always depicted in relation to cats. Sometimes she has the head of a cat or a lion, at others she is the cat carrying a sun. Many statues and pictures of cats are attributed to her, and she is often shown with cats or kittens at her feet.

The Egyptians revered their cats and often decorated them with golden earrings. When they died, they had them mummified and buried them in a special cats' cemetery.

Bast is sometimes portrayed beautifully clothed and wearing golden jewellery: she is very proud and sensual. She also represents 'warrior women' and is an important role model for women as she can be beautiful and tough, sensual and motherly. She always fulfils her responsibilities and still looks strong and attractive. She is a goddess to help us get up and go.

She is a moon deity when depicted with the head of a cat and in this aspect she is the goddess of singing and dancing and childbirth. She carries a basket and a ceremonial rattle.

When Bast wears a lion's head, she is the goddess of healing and the fertility of the earth; she is then a solar deity. Her bright eyes can turn to wrath if she is annoyed. She protects her father, the sun god Ra, from the serpent Alep.

Initially Bast was a local goddess in the Nile delta, but later she became very popular with all Egyptians. People would travel thousands of miles to honour her, at her sacred city of Bubastis. She is also a war goddess who protects the city.

Bast is an integrative goddess in her several aspects. She is both sun and moon. She is venerated for singing, dancing and childbirth, suggesting a ritualistic ceremony for giving birth. This is another reminder to be inclusive rather than either/or.

Above all, Bast is concerned with the enjoyment of life and the joy of music and dancing; bright colours and golden jewellery, feline movement and a certain wildness, which can turn to rage if crossed!

## A BAST MEDITATION

Does Bast speak to you as a goddess? Or is there another goddess animal or bird with which you have intuitive links? Meditate on the qualities of this creature in its natural surroundings. Capture it in images as a reminder of change in yourself. Bless these qualities. You may be starting a new journey after making some changes in your life. Allow your goddess to accompany you on the path and remember that Bast encourages enjoyment.

# Minerva & Athena, Andriamhilala & Cerridwen

## MINERVA

As a goddess of intelligence and creativity it seems appropriate that Minerva is also one of the mothers of the Muses. She is considered to be the 'personification of thinking, calculating and invention', (Ann and Imel, 1993) thus integrating factual thought with the creative thinking that is necessary for invention.

Athena, the Greek goddess of war.

There is a beautiful description of a boat that bore Minerva's robe as a sail, which was taken to the citadel to clothe her statue. A huge procession took place: people carried olive branches and young men wore wreaths of millet; virgins from the noble families carried baskets of offerings and the soldiers wore their armour. Everyone sang hymns honouring the goddess. Indeed it has been commented that Minerva's celebration brought together the academics and the workers.

Although she is closely identified with the Greek goddess Athena, it also has been suggested that Minerva did not have a warlike aspect until this fusion between the goddesses, and that originally, as patron of handicrafts, she was revered by ordinary people. However, Minerva's name comes from the word for 'mind', and there is no doubt that she was believed to have been the inventor of both music and musical instruments. Later her role was expanded when the Romans wanted to rename Sulis, the popular local healing water goddess in Bath, England, and she was called Sulis Minerva. We also find Minerva Medica, who was the patron of doctors.

## ATHENA

Athena is a war goddess who fights during wartime and is peaceful when there is no turbulence. It is said that she was born as an adult and sprang fully armed from the forehead of Zeus. She is one of the best-known virgin warrior goddesses. She is the protector of Athens and of other areas in Greece, although her ancient history suggests that she came from Crete. She is associated with snakes both in her domestic and her medical image.

The caduceus which Athena carries gives her yet another link with Minerva. Athena is responsible for the arts and literature as well as the practical arts, the latter probably linking with her history as a domestic goddess who looked after weavers, spinners and sewers.

Athena was the guide, often in the guise of an owl, when Odysseus was making his dangerous journey. She helped to rescue him from dangers but also acted as his conscience, with whom he would converse as he was making decisions. As well as the owl, her other emblems are the oak tree and the olive tree.

Minerva and Athena are both important goddesses for us today because they integrate the arts and the intellect, creativity and medicine. In modern thinking, the arts and sciences are often separated, and in many schools, pupils often have to make a choice between them at quite an early age. However, as these goddesses show us, art and science and art and medicine can be integrated and inspire each other. There lies healing.

## ADRIAMHILALA

Adriamhilala is a creator goddess from Madagascar, also known as Queen of Heaven, and she is thought to have given the first humans their flesh and their form (other deities supplying the rest of them). In one of her creation stories, humans are given the choice between eternal, renewable life or just the one life.

In ancient times, before the world was populated, the first people were told about birth and death and were given a choice about their ending. They could grow like the banana palm, which grows shoots that live on for future generations: the humans would have children that similarly would live on after they had died themselves. The other choice was to be like the moon, to die each month but then to be born each month, so they would live forever, but have no children. The humans chose to be like the banana.

*Cerridwen, allow me to know what I know, to understand what I need to know and to have courage to discover something new.*

## CERRIDWEN

Cerridwen is a Celtic goddess belonging to Wales and probably Cornwall. She is concerned with education, arts, knowledge, intelligence and creativity, as well as agriculture and magic. She is also named White Lady of Inspiration and Death. She is considered the patron of poetry, wisdom and grain. Some of her stories show her more terrifying aspect, such as the following tale of transformation and inspiration:

Cerridwen lived on an island in the middle of Lake Tegid. She had given birth to two children: a beautiful girl and a very ugly boy, Creidwy and Afagdu. She brewed a magical spell in her cauldron to make her son very intelligent and inspired. She kept her brew simmering for months on end, and when she had to go out she left it in the care of a mortal boy called Gwion. One day he spilt some onto his finger and sucked it; immediately he was able to understand everything going on around him. The past and the future were also unravelled to him, but he realized that Cerridwen would be angry so he ran away. She knew what had happened and gave chase, and both she and Gwion kept changing form to try and outrun each other: they changed from hare and greyhound, to fish and otter, to bird and hawk, and finally to grain and hen. At this stage she ate him and then gave birth to him. She threw him into the water, but he was rescued. He eventually grew up to be the greatest poet in the Welsh language.

Cerridwen's cauldron is considered to be never-ending; it will never be empty of her magical brew made up of six potent herbs. Her cauldron is called Amen: drinking its contents bestows inspiration and knowledge. Although Cerridwen has very frightening and dark aspects, her cauldron is a source of wisdom, inspiration and creativity.

## CERRIDWEN'S MAGICAL CAULDRON OF HEALING AND INSPIRATION

If you do not have a cauldron, choose a soup pot or similar container, then decide whether you wish to undertake this exercise in your house or

outdoors. You can make your potion in your kitchen or on an outside fire.

If you can, pick fresh herbs. Take a selection of rosemary, thyme, mint and sage (or any other aromatic herbs that you like), and crush them into a cauldron of hot water. Allow it to come to a gentle simmer with plenty of steam. Ensure the cauldron is stable, so you do not get scalded by steam or water. Sit comfortably and upright, on a stool or the ground, or on a high stool if you are using the kitchen stove.

Close your eyes and gently breathe in the steam and the aromas, and then breathe out again. Focus on your life now and any difficulties that you need to resolve. Choose just one of these difficulties and let it 'float in the steam'. Let Cerridwen inspire you with a solution that perhaps you can write down as a story or a poem. Let all the goddesses of the arts give you the courage to take the risk of moving on creatively. Give thanks for inspiration and courage.

A DANCE TO CERRIDWEN
Cerridwen can be venerated at a group ritual and honoured with offerings and dance. A cauldron of flowers floating on water is placed in the middle of the circle. Invite people to dance in the circle while focusing on the floating flowers. Everyone then drinks wine and eats cakes and continues dancing in joyous celebration. Feel blessed by the company of friends and enjoy their special qualities.

# Grandmother Spider

Grandmother Spider shares many attributes with Spider Woman and other creator-deities of various Native American groups. Grandmother Spider is weaving new creations with her spider's web. She brought many gifts to the Native Americans, including language.

One tradition recounts that Grandmother Spider started as an underworld deity who then led humans into the world and brought them light. Another view is that she was an ancient earth goddess who brought light and fire to humans by

PUT YOUR FEET DOWN WITH POLLEN
PUT YOUR HANDS DOWN WITH POLLEN
PUT YOUR HEAD DOWN WITH POLLEN
YOUR FEET ARE POLLEN
YOUR HANDS ARE POLLEN, YOUR BODY IS POLLEN
YOUR MIND IS POLLEN, YOUR VOICE IS POLLEN
THE TRAIL IS BEAUTIFUL, BE STILL

breaking off a piece of the sun. As a deity associated with thinking and transformation she 'illuminated' the world for humans.

Grandmother Spider taught the human race how to make pottery, how to make bows and arrows, and how to weave bowstrings. She also brought the alphabet to her people by weaving it in her web and so developed language.

Another story tells how the twins Nayanezgani and Thoradzistshini discovered Grandmother Spider in the underworld by seeing her smoke rising from the ground. She welcomed the twins, who one day said that they wanted to travel to meet their father. She told them that the journey was long and dangerous, but they would not be dissuaded, so she created this chant (left) to protect them whenever they encountered danger from a live eagle. Pollen is considered sacred by the Native Americans. She also gave them two 'life-feathers', which are tail feathers from a live eagle.

The twins survived their journey, as well as all the dangerous tests that their father put them through before he finally accepted them as his sons.

## GRANDMOTHER SPIDER'S CHANT OF PEACE

Grandmother Spider's chant has a very soothing rhythm. Read it over several times to yourself and feel the rhythmic beat. Start to tap the beat and let it into your whole body. Move around the room saying the chant to yourself and see how this chant creates earth-based movement. Let it transform into a celebration of your strength and calm. Join with others to create your own ritual of calm and peace inspired by Grandmother Spider.

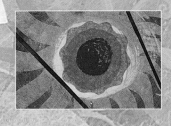

It is important to remind yourself that you are a creative and artistic person and that you have a lot of knowledge. However old you are, you have number of years of experience. These exercises will help you strengthen your creativity and knowledge. The goddesses reassure us that we are creative and that we do have knowledge – and that one enhances the other.

### WEB WATCHING

Get up early in the morning, just about dawn, and see the spiders' webs that have been created during the night. They can be in the smallest of gardens, in the grasses or plants or on the washing line and the posts. They sparkle with dew, or with hoar-frost if it is very cold, and create a magical atmosphere. Just take some time to look at this natural creation; perhaps it will assist you to create your own web. Remember Arachne, who was condemned to weave forever because she dared to criticize the gods. Do we need to find the strength to challenge authority? Perhaps we do not need to compete like Arachne but maybe we need some strength from Grandmother Spider's chant.

Remember that children find spiders' webs quite wonderful, so give them an opportunity to see and tell stories about different webs. If they express any fears quite openly, without fear of ridicule, their dreamcatcher will work more effectively for them. After all, Spider Man is a positive and protective hero: maybe he could be a good starting point. It is important to tell children goddess stories from an

### CREATING A DREAMCATCHER FOR YOURSELF

You may already own a dreamcatcher – a web of threads woven on a wooden hoop, with a black bead near the centre to represent Grandmother Spider. Usually feathers and personal items are hung from the bottom of the ring and the top has a means for hanging it up. Hang your dreamcatcher near your window and enjoy calmer sleep. The spider in the dreamcatcher intercepts all our dreams, and devours the nightmares and bad dreams but allows the good dreams through. If you do not have a dreamcatcher, then paint your own on a large piece of paper. Paint in the web and hang from it things that have a special meaning to you. Create a story of a possible dream that your dreamcatcher may know and read it aloud. Perhaps use this picture as a pattern to make your own dreamcatcher, and learn how to weave a web.

early age, to draw pictures and keep a scrap-book. This is a resource that will inspire them, especially in their creative and artistic work.

## SYMBOLS OF STRENGTH

Remember how Grandmother Spider gave the twins two 'life-feathers' to guard them from danger – feathers from the eagle, an enormous, fearsome bird. What power can you harness to stop you feeling fear – maybe from an animal totem, maybe from something strong in the wilderness?

## CREATING A MANDALA

Take a large piece of paper and draw a circle the size of a dinner plate. Use a mug to draw an inner circle, and then divide the outer circle into four segments without crossing the inner circle. The inner circle represents your core beliefs, whether a religion, a philosophy or code of ethics. The top left-hand segment represents your guide(s), who or what guides you through life; it may indeed be one or more of the goddesses. The top right-hand segment represents the

things you are good at – your skills and training and experience. The bottom-right-hand segment is for your fears or what makes you vulnerable, and the bottom left is for your creativity and artistry. Fill in the five spaces using painting or drawing or writing, or single words, or a combination of all of them. Decorate it in whatever way you like, so that you are making a picture as well as a statement. This is a holistic representation of yourself, right now. Take time to reflect on your picture and see which of the segments can help each other. For example, can the guide help the fears? Or the creativity enhance the skills? What is missing from your picture and which aspect can help you discover it?

The word 'mandala' is Sanskrit for 'whole'. Many Indian and Tibetan mandalas tell stories and make statements about epic moments in people's lives. Your first mandala is one of discovery, and new ideas can come from it. You may like to make a mandala about your journey through life, which is the very essence of this section of the book.

# JOURNEY THROUGH THIS BOOK

At the beginning of the book I asked you to prepare yourself for a journey. Perhaps you had already begun that preparation without realising it, before your contact with this book. Had you had a dream of new beginnings? Nothing is a coincidence, and as you have journeyed through the different stories and exercises, think about the times when you have paused and given yourself time to reflect.

Maybe there is a story or myth that stays with you, which, like a dream, comes back with different meanings. There could be an exercise that you found difficult and want to try again with a fresh perspective.

This book is both a story-book and a healing text, and the various reflections, chants and exercises are there to help you bring about the changes you wish for in your life. Some of the exercises are for you to undertake alone; others you can share with friends, family and children. You may develop your own variations of the exercises – discover your own path for the journey, and treat what is offered as a series of signposts.

When you have finished the book, look through the Goddess Book of Life you have created for yourself, which will show your dreams, ideas reflections and the new directions

you have taken. There will probably be gaps when you chose not to write or draw, and there may be other times when ideas tumbled out of you. Perhaps you wrote your very first poem, or took the risk of creating with paints.

Give yourself time to decide how to implement the possible changes you would like to make. Maybe there is a group of you who could meet together and support each other in your new directions. You may need practical help in making changes to

your house or your garden. Have you chosen one goddess as your guide or are there several who inspire you? Create a blessed goddess space where you can reflect and meditate.

Allow your senses to be fully connected to your experiences. You may find after journeying through this book that colours become more vivid, smells more acute, sounds much clearer and textures more vital. Always allow time to give blessings to your activity, your tools, your ideas and your creativity.

BLESSING TO THE NEW JOURNEY
BLESSING IN THE SPECIAL QUEST
BLESSING WITH THE LETTING GO OF OLD WAYS
BLESSING FOR
THE SMALL THINGS THAT MAKE A DIFFERENCE

BLESSED BE

Goddess of the pathways, allow me to be guided, allow me to be a guide. Let my path lead me to the riches of your wisdom.

The end of one journey is the beginning of another. A creative journey through this book also means a journey through ourselves. A personal journey through our inner life reflects the outer journey through the creative experience: we never return to the place where we started. Some experiences will not have touched us and others will make us stop in our tracks and ponder. We will see a landscape with a choice of pathways, the old ways and the new. Maybe the way ahead is not completely clear and we need time to wait or to test our intuition.

Many of the goddesses in this book can help us in the very process of choices and we may need to go back again and look at what they can give us. For example Ariadne can support our stargazing and Olwen allows us to have a flowered path; Pele gives us permission for our anger and Demeter allows us to grieve.

Let this book and all the creative ideas you have written in your own Goddess Book of Life support you to let go of an unhelpful past and stay in a more creative present. Eventually they will guide you to a more fulfilling future.

You may decide to go on a new journey, a pilgrimage to new places or a visit to some of the places we have shared in this book. Many of the goddesses have sites where we can experience their ancient history and their presence as a reality. Enjoy the journey as well as the arrival, and always remember to give thanks.

It will be for you to decide if you wish to make this journey on your own or with like-minded pilgrims. My own journey started in the heart of Transylvania where I discovered the goddess Bendis and the Roma healing traditions. The energy of the wolves has given me new perspectives and allowed me to make major changes in my life.

You will have your own landscape, your own journey, your own dreams and stories.

Let it be your decision, with guidance from the goddesses, to make changes and plan future directions. If you need to pause and reflect for even longer, take it as a blessing to stand still for a while.

One journey will lead to another with pauses and reflections in between. Trust your intuition and follow the flow and be blessed. All is well and all will be well.

*Allow the goddess to enter your heart and give you a new direction*
*Allow the goddess to take you on a journey for a special quest*
*Allow the goddess to remind you of the small things that get overlooked*

Let there be peace in my HEART and a LIGHT on my path.

Let me give THANKS.

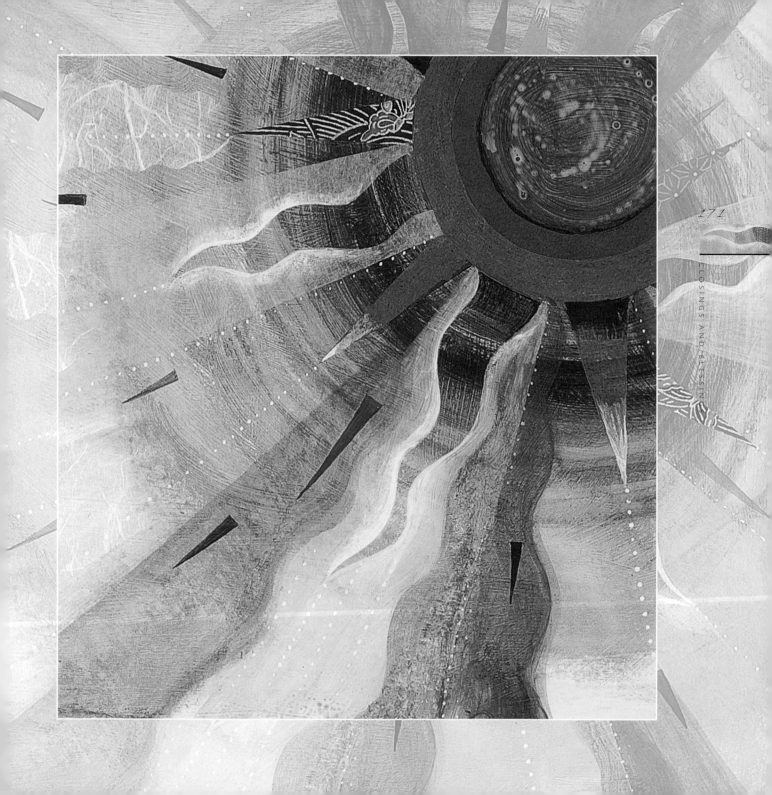

Aeschylus, *The Oresteia*,
Penguin Classic edition.
1979
Ann, M and Imel, D M,
*Goddesses in World
Mythology*, Oxford
University Press, 1993
Baring, A and Cashford, J
*The Myth of the
Goddess*, Arkana/Penguin,
London, 1993
Begg I, *The Cult of the Black

Virgin*, Penguin, London,
1996
Benard E and B Moon,
*Goddesses Who Rule*,
Oxford University Press,
2000
Brinton, Perera S, *Descent
to the Goddess*, Inner City
Books, Toronto, 1981
Bryant P, *The Native
American Mythology*,
Aquarian Guide, Harper,

London, 1991
Campbell J, *The Masks of
God, Volume 1: Primitive
Mythology*, Souvenir Press,
London, 2000
Campbell J, *The Masks of
God, Volume 11: Oriental
Mythology*, Souvenir Press,
London, 2000
Cambell J, *The Masks of
God, Volume 111:
Occidental Mythology*,

Souvenir Press, London,
2001
Carey K, *Return of the Bird
Tribes*, Harper, San
Francisco, 1988
Davies M, *Lore of the
Sacred Horse*, Capall
Bann, Chieveley, 1995
Dixon-Kennedy M, *Native
American Myth and
Legend*, Blandford Press,
London, 1996

Farrar J and S and G Bone, *The Complete Dictionary of European Gods and Goddesses*, Capall Bann, Chieveley, 2000

Farrar J and V Russell, *The Magical History of the Horse*, Capall Bann, Chieveley, 1999

Gantz J (translator), *The Mabinogion*, Penguin, London, 1976

Gersie A, *Storymaking in Bereavement*, Jessica Kingsley, London, 1991

Gersie A, *Earthtales: Storytelling in Times of Change*, Greenprint, London, 1992

Gimbutas M, *The Living Goddesses*, University of California Press, California, 1999

Gimbutas M, *The Language of the Goddess*, Thames and Hudson, London, 2001

Goodison L and C Morris, *Ancient Goddesses*, British Museum Press, London, 1998

Graves R, *The White Goddess*, Faber and Faber, Manchester, 1948/1997

Husain S, *The Goddess: Power, Sexuality and the Feminine Divine*, Harper, London, 1997

Jennings S, *Theatre, Ritual and Transformation*, Routledge, London, 1995

Jennings S, *Introduction to Dramatherapy: Ariadne's Ball of Thread*, Jessica Kingsley, London, 1998

Jennings S, *Introduction to Developmental Playtherapy: Playing and Health*, Jessica Kingsley, London, 1999

Jennings S, *Pocket Goddess 1, Brigid: Fertility, Creativity and Healing*, Rowan, Glastonbury, 2000

Jennings S, *Pocket Goddess 2, Inanna: Journey into Darkness and Light*, Rowan, Glastonbury, 2001

Jennings S, 'Re-stage Your Life', Avalon Journal, Winter, 2002

Kipling R, *A Tree Song*, London Dent/Everyman, 1998

Lurker M, *Dictionary of Gods and Goddesses, Devils and Demons*, Routledge, London, 2000

Monaghan P, *The Goddess Within*, Llewellyn Publications, St Pauls MN, 1999

Monaghan P, *The New Book of Goddesses and Heroines*, Llewellyn, St Pauls MN, 2000

Neumann E, (trans Manheim) *The Great Mother*, Mythos, Duncan Baird, Princeton/Bollingen, 1991

Radice B, *Who's Who in the Ancient World*, Penguin, London, 1985

Rasmussen K 'Across Artic America', *Report of the Fifth Thule Expedition*, 1921-24

Redgrove P, *The Black Goddess and the Sixth Sense*, Palladin, London, 1989

Rees E *Christian Symbols, Ancient Roots*, Jessica Kingsley, London, 1988

Saunders N J, *Animal Spirits*, Duncan Baird, London, 1995

Shakespeare, William, *A Midsummer Night's Dream, Hamlet, King Lear, Cymbeline, Henry V, Macbeth, The Tempest, Anthony and Cleopatra, Romeo and Juliet, Two Gentlemen of Verona*, New Penguin Shakespeare

Synder C, *Exploring the World of King Arthur*, London, Thames and Hudson, 2000

Walker B G, *The Woman's Encyclopedia of Myths and Secrets*, Harper, San Francisco, 1983

Yeats WB 'The Wandering Aeneas', Dent/Everyman, London, 1997

# INDEX

*Figures in italics indicate illustrations*

Adam 62
Adriamhilala 161-2, *161*
Adrika 27
Aeneas 78
Aeschylus: *Agamemnon*
  86
Afagdu 162
Ahurani 148
Aigle 146
Ainu peoples 12
Air 8, 52-65, 156
  goddesses 54-63
  stories and exercises
  64-5
Airmed 146-7, *147*
Ama-terasu-o-mi-kami
  102-3, *102*, 108
Amazons 86
Ame-no-sade-yori-hime
  143
Anahita 89-90, *89*, 91
Anat 132
Anath 42
Aoede 121
Aphrodite 70, 78
Apsarases 27
Arachne 166
Araentsic 55
Arberth 92
Ariadne 66, 70, 71, 74, *75*,
  81
Arianrhod 88, *88*, 90,
  106
Artemis 12, 86, *87*, 147
Arthur, King 106, 118
Arundhati 129, *129*
Ashera 42, *43*
Asklepius 146
Astarte 132
Atargatis 132-3, *132*
Ate 132
Athena 146, 160-61, *160*,
  160
Avalokita 70
Avalon 41, 133

Baal 42
Badb 118-19
Bahia, Brazil 33
Balder 60
Bast 18-19, 158, *159*
Beiwe 104, *104*, 105
Beiwe-Neida 104
Beltane 31, 32, 130
Bendis 88-9, *89*
Benin people 84
Bernard of Clairvaux,
  St 45
Black Madonna 44-7
Black Virgin of Chatillon
  45
Bona Dea 130
Botticelli, Sandro:
  *The Birth of Venus* 78
Brigantes 20
Brigid (Bride, Brig) 12, 20,
  *21*, 22, 23, 114, 142,
  143, 147, 150, 156
Burning Bush, chapel of
  the, Mount Sinai 12
Bush People 76

Caer Arianrhod 88
Cailleach 22
Cailleach Beara 156-7
Calliope 121
Canaan 42
Candlemas 150
Cardea 60-61
Carmenae 147
Cerridwen 111, 162-3,
  *162*
Chengkai, Old Mother 26
Chief-who-holds-the-
  earth 55
Chullwch 106
Clio 121
Coatlicue 46
Cordelia 31-2, *31*
creativity and knowledge
  154-67

goddesses 156-65
stories and exercises
  166-7
Creidwy 162
Cronus 40
Cybele 44, 45
Cyclops 40

Dahomean Moon Woman
  84
Danu 157
De Danaan 157
De Danaan, Tuatha 157
  death cults 60
Demeter 114, 116, *117*,
  122, 128
Dian Cecht 146
Diana 86, *87*, 147
Diana, Princess 86
Dionysus 74, 88, 89
Dou Mou 143
  dreamcatcher 166
Dumuzi 72
Dylan 88
Dzelarhons 13

Earth 8, 38-51, 156
  goddesses 40-49
  stories and exercises
  50-51
eggs 64
Egle, Queen of the
  Serpents 27
Elegba 26
elements 6, 8, 9, 156;
  *see also* Air; Earth; Fire;
  Water
Endymion 90
Enki 72, 80, 81
Epona 30, *30*, 31
Erato 121
Ereshkigal 72, 80
Erinyes 41
Estanatlehi (Changing
  Woman) 114-15, *115*

Etain 147
Euterpe 121
Evening Star 157
Evening Star Woman 76,
  76
Eveningstar 71

Fauna 130
fertility and childbirth
  126-39
  goddesses 128-37
  stories and exercises
  138-9
Festival of Candles 86
Fire 10-23, 156
  goddesses 12-21
  stories and exercises
  22-3
firebird motif 99
Flora 41
Formorii 157
Fox Moon goddess 98
Freya 56, *57*, 98
Frigg 56, 60
Fuji 12, *12*

Gaia 40, 128
Ganesh 135
Ganga 147
Gilgamesh 62
Glastonbury 41
gLu-ma Ghirdhima 13,
  156
Goddess Book of Life 6
Goleuddydd 106
Grandmother Spider 156,
  164, *165*, 166, 167
Great Plains Indians 103
Great Spirit 76
Green Goddess 130
Green Man 31, 130
Griselicae Nymphae 147
Guatemalan 'worry dolls'
  81
Gusts-of-wind 55

Gwion 162
Gwydian 88

Hades 116
Haïda people 13
Han (Black of Darkness)
  98
Harpies 60, *60*
Hathor 19, 136, *137*
Haumea 14
healing 140-53
  goddesses 142-51
  stories and exercises
  152-3
hearth 16, 17, 20
Heavenly Bodies 6
Hecate 12, 114, 116, *117*
Hestia 16
Hexe, Die 148, *148*, 149
Hina 84-5
Hine ahuone 58
Hine nui te po 58
Hine titama 58-9, *58*
Holst, Gustav: *The Planets*
  70, 78
Homer: *Hymn to Artemis*
  86
Horus 28, 45, 74
Hygeia 146
Hyrokkin 59-60, *59*, 61

Ilmater 54, 64, 65
Imbolc, feast of 20
Inanna 62, 70, 72, *73*,
  80-81
Inuit people 19, 34, 54-5
Iroquois 55
Ishtar 62, 132
Isis 28, *29*, 36-7, *37*, 44,
  45, 74
Ixlexwani 54

Jehovah 62
Jeremiah 42
Jesus Christ 12, 20, 114

Jonah 132
Juks-Akka 134

Kadlu 55
Kali 122, 143,
Kilauea, Hawaii 13, 14
  knowledge see creativity
  and knowledge
Kuan Yin 144, 145
Kweeto 55

Laima 12
Lakota tribe 48
Lakshmi 122
Lilith 59, 62, 63, 65
Lleu 88
Llyr 31

Macha 118, 118, 119
Macumba cult 33
Madonna of Monserrat,
  Spain 45
Maia 130, 131
mandala 167
Mars 70, 78
Mary, the Virgin 12, 114,
  130
Mary Magdalene 114
Mary the Mother of
  James 114
Maui 58-9
May Day 31, 130
Maya 103-4, 103
Melete 121
Meliae 41
Melisai 86
Molla 112, 142
Melpomene 121
mental ill-health 104, 105
Merlin 118
Miach 146
Milky Way 71
Mineme 121
Minerva 44, 45, 160, 160,
  161

Minerva Medica 150
Minos, King of Crete 74
Minotaur 66, 74
Moon 66, 70, 71, 82-95
  goddesses 84-93
  stories and exercises
  94-5
Mordred 118
Morgan Le Faye 118
Morning Star 103
Morningstar 71
Morrigan 118-19
Mot 42
Muses 120-21, 121, 156,
  160

Naayanxatisei
  (Whirlwind Woman) 54
Namaka 14
Navaho people 114, 115
Naya peoples 143
Nayanezgani 164
Nemain 118, 119
Nemetona 119
Nephthys 74
Niarimamau (Wind
  Woman) 54
Nile River 28
Ninshubar 72, 80
Norns 120, 120
Nut 74, 74, 76

Obatala 26
Odin 56
Odysseus 161
Ogma 147
Olwen 106, 107
Ona people 70
Ops 130
Orkney Isles 60, 61
Orpheus 88, 146
Oshun 26, 26, 148
Osiris 28, 36, 37, 74
Our Lady of Guadalupe
  44, 46-7

Pachamama (Mama
  Pacha) 47, 47
Panacea 146, 146
Parvati 134-5, 135
Pawnee First Woman 157
Pele 13, 14, 15, 19
Persephone 114, 116, 117
Phosphorus 12
Pleiades 71
Polymnia 121
Pomona 41, 41
Pontus 40
Poseidon 74
Pretannic Isles 132, 133
Priapos 17
Pwyll, Prince 92
Pyramus 128, 129

Ra 19, 28, 74, 76, 136
Rhiannon 92, 93
Rigantona 92, 133
Rome: Circus Maximus 78

Saami people 134
Saga 156
Saintes-Maries-de-la-Mer,
  Camargue 114
Santiago de Compostela,
  Spain 45
Sar-Akka 134
Sara 46, 114
Sarasvati 122
Saule 98, 98
Sedna 34, 35
Segeta 147
Sekhmet 18-19, 18, 23,
  136
Selene 90
Sequana 147
Serer people 84
Set 36, 74
Shakespeare, William 44;
  Henry V 120-21; King
  Lear 32; Macbeth 120,
  149; A Midsummer

Night's Dream 121,
  128-9
Shakti 122, 123, 143
Shinto people 102
Shiva 134-5
Shu 76
Silbury Hill, Wiltshire 150
Skan 98
Skuld 120
Sophia 100, 101
Spider Man 166
Spring of Juturna 16
Star Women 76-7, 77
stars 66, 68-81
  goddesses 70-79
  stories and exercises
  80-1
Suilohead 150
Sul, Sulis 147, 150, 151,
  160
Sulis Minerva 150, 160
Suliviae 150
Sun 66, 70-84, 96-109;
  goddesses 98-107;
  stories and exercises
  108-9
Surya 98
Susa-no-o 102, 108
swan symbol 99

Tane Mahuta 58
Tara 70, 71
Temiar people 26-7, 134
Terpsichore 121
Thalia 121
Therma 147
Thermaia 147
Thermia 147
Theseus 66, 74
Thisbe 128-9
Thoradzistshini 164
Thracians 88-9
Thunderbird 76
Tii 84
Titans 40

Tree of Life 40, 42, 115
Triple Goddesses 110,
  112-25, 150
  stories and exercises
  124-5

Uke-Mochi 108
Uks Akka 134, 134,
  139
Urania 121
Uranus 40
Urd 120
Uvavnuk 12, 19, 19

Valkyries 56
Venus 78, 79
Verdandi 120
Vesta 16-17, 16, 19
Vestal Virgins 16, 17, 147
Vinalia Priora festival 78

Water 8, 24-37, 156
  goddesses 26-35
  stories and exercises
  36-7
White Buffalo Calf
  Woman 48, 49, 50-51
White Horse, Uffington
  30
wisdom 6
witches 148-9
Wyrd Sisters 120

Yemaya 32-3, 32
Yggdrasil (the World
  Tree) 120
Yoruba people 26, 32-3
Ysbaddeden 106
Yuletide 96

Zeus 160

175

INDEX

GODDESSES

# ACKNOWLEDGEMENTS

I would like to give thanks to all my friends and family, especially my grandchildren who have inspired and supported me through the writing of this book. Ideas and creative approaches have been influenced by so many people that I cannot separate them as individuals. There are some people I must thank personally: Dan and Luminitsa for being wonderful new friends, Sheila and Jim for feeding me, Sue Hall for surviving all the computer crashes, Stuart Booth for support all the way through, Elektra Tselikas for being a real friend, Alida Gersie for inspired talks, Anna Chesner for her capacity to make me laugh, and Suzanne Redding for her unfailing friendship. Pauline Royce is my special Glastonbury friend who has inspired so many ideas.

**Hay House, Inc., P.O. Box 5100, Carlsbad, CA 92018-5100**

**(760) 431-7695** or **(800) 654-5126**
**(760) 431-6948 (fax)** or **(800) 650-5115 (fax)**
**www.hayhouse.com**

**Published and distributed in Australia by:**
Hay House Australia Pty. Ltd. • 18/36 Ralph St.
Alexandria NSW 2015 • *Phone:* 612-9669-4299
*Fax:* 612-9669-4144 • www.hayhouse.com.au

**Published and distributed in the United Kingdom by:**
Hay House UK, Ltd. • Unit 62, Canalot Studios
222 Kensal Rd., London W10 5BN
*Phone:* 44-20-8962-1230 • *Fax:* 44-20-8962-1239
www.hayhouse.co.uk

**Published and distributed in the
Republic of South Africa by:**
Hay House SA (Pty), Ltd., P.O. Box 990, Witkoppen 2068
*Phone/Fax:* 2711-7012233 • orders@psdprom.co.za

**Distributed in Canada by:**
Raincoast • 9050 Shaughnessy St., Vancouver, B.C. V6P 6E5
*Phone:* (604) 323-7100 • *Fax:* (604) 323-2600